MW00873777

CONTENTS

Rabble Rouser Rising	1
The Mayor Slayer!	2
Chapter 1	4
Chapter 2	11
Chapter 3	21
Chapter 4	38
Chapter 5	51
Chapter 6	76
Chapter 7	97
Chapter 8	109
Chapter 9	128
Chapter 10	140
Chapter 11	154
Chapter 12	159
Chapter 13	170
Chapter 14	184
Chapter 15	194
Chapter 16	210
Chapter 17	235
Chapter 18	244

RABBLE ROUSER
RISING

To Andrew and
Tani,

from

[signature]

1

THE MAYOR SLAYER!

By Patrick Duff

Chapter 1: The Birth Of The Rabble Rouser
Chapter 2: Getting Circled By A Blackhawk
Chapter 3: Fireworks & Shovels
Chapter 4: Duff Deposes Delran
Chapter 5: The Receipts
Chapter 6: The Shakedown
Chapter 7: Hit Blogs & Lawsuits
Chapter 8: So Long Sal
Chapter 9: Senile Or A Liar
Chapter 10: Blogger Busted & Bids Were Split
Chapter 11: Post Delran Debacle Breakdown
Chapter 12: The Bat Signal Above Medford
Chapter 13: Karen By Design
Chapter 14: Beer Drinking Chuck
Chapter 15: The $10,000 Fine
Chapter 16: That Kingdom Where No One Likes The King
Chapter 17: It's Good To Be The Mayor's Friend
Chapter 18: What Happens Now

The following is a collection of select articles that are in chronological order of when they were printed on my Rabble Rouser site. Additionally there are minutes and transcripts from the municipal meetings where myself and others spoke, which are also in chronological order, as well as the breakdowns of each chapter and new stories of my life. This is also an educational book for those who are interested in being their own hometown Rabble Rouser. This is the true story about my deep dive into exposing corruption in my hometown of Delran, and in the town of Medford. Everything is true, nothing is embellished except for the third to the last sentence of this book. But you better not go read it right now like I would.   Please, enjoy the show first.

If you like what you read please leave me a review on Amazon.

Rabble Rouse : to stir up public sentiment by emotionalism.

CHAPTER 1

The Birth Of The Rabble Rouser

On January 28th, 1986 I faked a sore belly to get out of elementary school class so I could sit in the nurse's office to watch the Challenger take off with Christa McAuliffe aboard. She was a teacher who was selected to be the first American civilian to go into space. Only she never made it. As the nurse and I watched the shuttle explode into a thousand pieces, the nurse became visibly upset, but I can vividly remember having the uncontrollable urge to want to break the bad news to my entire class in what would be my first big story as a reporter.

I bolted from the nurse's office and barged into my fourth grade class knowing that what I was about to say would be the key to stopping the torture of that day's English lesson for a kid like myself dealing with ADHD and Dyslexia. And it worked. What I said at that moment changed the entire pattern of class by creating a bit of chaos, which is an environment that I thrive in. It wasn't my normal fart joke, or funny noise that made people want to listen to me. It was my first real scoop, and it felt amazing!

I began njrabblerouser.com because the media in the Philadelphia area, especially in South Jersey, are completely controlled by the people that they are meant to report on. The very first story I published on April 26th, 2018 on my Rabble Rouser Blog was regarding a Starbucks in Philadelphia where two black men were removed and arrested by police for merely waiting for a friend. A Starbucks employee had asked the two if she could help them, and when they said no and sat down to wait for their friend before ordering, she called the cops.

As soon as I listened to the 911 call from the incident, I knew something was off. The caller sounded like she was calling for a pizza, which made me think this wasn't the first time a call like that was made. So I made a Right-to-Know request to the Philly Police Department, seeking the 911 logs from that store's address, located in one of Philly's ritziest neighborhoods. What I found blew me away.

Those police logs showed that 58 calls were made to 911 from that Starbucks in just a 15 month period. And even more alarming, 28 of those calls were made in just 2017 alone to have people removed. The 911 call to have police remove those two men in April, 2018 was made by the then manger of that Starbucks store. That police removal triggered a massive scandal that eventually impacted all Starbucks stores in America. The female manager whose 911 call caused that scandal was immediately fired once the international news descended on Philadelphia. But with that high number of 911 calls being made in such a short period of time, and from the same posh Rittenhouse Square location, one had to ask themselves, what the heck was really happening there, and why?

I immediately shared the information I discovered with an editor at *The Philadelphia Inquirer*, the largest newspaper in the city. That editor, David Preston, said he was excited about my information, 'news' that all other reporters had missed, including reporters from national TV networks and reporters from international news outlets. Preston promised me he would assign a reporter to investigate what I had discovered and have it delivered to him ASAP.

Well, for two weeks Preston beat around the bush. I stayed in touch with him about the status of his promised investigation until he all but went silent. He refused to answer my emails.

No *Inquirer* reporter ever called me. Preston officially killed my story. But I wasn't giving up.

I reached out to several media outlets, and the startling information I had uncovered was finally picked up by The Root.com on May 11th, 2018, who ran a story titled "It turns out, that cop-calling Starbucks manager might just be the Beckiest Becky who ever Beckied". The Root is an African American oriented online magazine launched in 2008 by Henry Louis Gates Junior and Donald E. Graham.

I then reached out to *The Philadelphia Tribune* newspaper, which is also an African American centered publication, and on May 14, 2018 the *Tribune* ran a front page story titled Uptick in 911 calls for Starbucks manager, crediting my research, and landing me an interview on the NewsMakers program featured on Philadelphia's KYW news radio with Cherri Gregg. Since Gregg is also African American, it seemed the main stream media, which is geared mostly towards white people, didn't want Starbucks to look even worse. So I am guessing that instead of The Inquirer having a reporter contact Starbucks to seek comment on the controversial story, they had their best sales representative contact them instead to see if they'd like to "buy" advertisements.

Over the next couple of years I wrote about my groundbreaking research about the legendary Dr. Martin Luther King Jr. That research discovered new information about King's very first protest - held in New Jersey - that all major historians of King had missed the true significance for decades. When I found out that King planned that protest from a home in Camden, I filed to have the home placed on the National Register of Historic Places with the State of NJ. Incredibly, the New Jersey State Historic Preservation Office doesn't see my discoveries about MLK, the home, or the protest as worthy of recognition even though people like MLK's confidant Congressman John Lewis did. This dismissal by NJ's Preservation Office is a whole 'nother book' in itself, only it's stuck in edit. I wrote about the former Mayor of Point Pleasant Beach, Stephen Reid, and how that small town NJ official was lobbying for an anti-marijuana group, but doing so unregistered, blatantly breaking the law. That story made it into NJ.COM and High Times Magazine, and also made it so Reid badly lost his next election to a fellow Council person, Paul Kanitra, who is still the Mayor as of 2024.

At the beginning of 2019 I opened Philadelphia's first legal cannabis smoking lounge, which was featured on the front page of the Philadelphia Inquirer, and somehow made its way to Fox News and other national media outlets. I partnered with a great doctor and began throwing events to provide large groups of people with their medical cannabis certifications in one spot, and have a little fun while people are waiting with food, comedy, music or the use of our lounge to indulge in dabs and bong rips.

When COVID-19 hit everything changed for my lounge. Nobody was coming to get their doctors certifications in person, and surely nobody was coming in to smoke with each other. Like my lounge, passing to the left, was something also killed by COVID. So I immediately began lobbying the Governor of Pennsylvania and Assembly persons to have the law changed in the state to allow for medical cannabis doctor certifications over the phone, and roughly a week later, they changed the law.

As soon as the COVID restrictions started, I knew something was really wrong with the story. I mean, why were they closing down the world over a coronavirus, which from the studies I could find, are as common as the cold, because it is the common cold. I knew right away that we were either dealing with a man made bioweapon, or a man made hoax, and I printed my first article questioning the pandemic just a week after the lockdowns started.

Patient Zero, Wuhan or Wanaque? 3-23-20

The first cases of the novel Coronavirus, (known officially as COVID-19) were reported to the World Health Organization on December 31st of 2019 by the Chinese Government. Since then the virus has spread across every continent except for Antarctica, and it did so in just a couple of months.

In an unprecedented set of moves, entire states have forced businesses to close. The Governor of New Jersey Phil Murphy, even imposed a curfew, as if the virus is somehow more susceptible to spreading at night.

Some Chinese officials have claimed that the virus was deliberately released by the U.S. Army by an Army team that was in Wuhan to compete in the Military World Games in October 2019. U.S. President Donald Trump dismissed that claim from Chinese officials as ridiculous, even citing that claim as defense against charges that he was engaging in racism by publicly referring to COVID-19 as the "Chinese Virus" or "Kung Flu".

That Chinese claim, made in a tweet, went on to ask America to identify its patient zero, as if America was hiding where the outbreak actually started. That U.S. Army team is said to have eaten at the fish market in Wuhan that scientists are claiming that COVID-19 was born. But was it?

The fact that top Chinese officials made such an accusation sure brought out the old conspiracy theorist in me. That and other factors like America's financial markets were tanking and we were under the closest version of martial law since Japanese-Americans were moved into internment camps by the federal government during WWII.

The federal government's Picatinny Arsenal is located in far northern New Jersey and it houses ARDEC. This entity is the division of the Army responsible for making and improving new weapons, including for bio-warfare.

Just 25 miles from the arsenal sits the Wanaque Center for Nursing and Rehabilitation. This is a facility center for nursing and rehabilitation whose patients include children who are medically fragile or receiving palliative care.

The Wanaque Center made major headlines in 2018 when 11 children under care at the facility died from an outbreak of the adenovirus, and more than 30 were sickened.

In January of 2020 Wanaque was back in the news after an investigation into a large number of children, along with an elderly patient, were again sickened in December of 2019.

However this time, the infection event at Wanaque was with a Coronavirus.

Which type of Coronavirus that caused the 2019 infection at the facility is not known, since there are several types of this virus, but the timing arguably raised questions, especially considering the area around the center had a much higher COVID-19 infection rate than the rest of the country. The town of Teaneck, New Jersey sits just 20 miles from the Wanaque Center where that outbreak was reported in December, and is only 50 miles from New Rochelle NY, where the city had been on lock-down for weeks with the news reporting that over 100 people were infected.

During that December 2019 outbreak at the Wanaque facility, the children got better, but the center refused to comment on the elderly patient's condition, which is still unknown. (NorthJersey.com is the only news organization to provide coverage on that 2019 Coronavirus incident at Wanaque.)

A curious circumstance: one of the workers at Wanaque also tested positive for the virus but was not asked to quarantine. Even more alarming, none of the facility's nurses or aides who worked with the sick were quarantined. So it's reasonable to assume that many Wanaque workers could have easily carried that Coronavirus back to their local communities without even knowing it. Remember, workers at Wanaque live in the surrounding areas like Teaneck, which is in the heart of Bergen County, and ground zero for the virus in NJ with some of the highest infection rates..

The first news reports to hit the U.S. about COVID-19 were on January 9th of 2020, just six days after the New Jersey Department of Health reportedly closed its case on a Coronavirus outbreak at the Wanaque Center.

So the question must be asked: was patient zero for COVID-19 someone in Wuhan, or was it possibly a person 7,452-miles away near Wanaque?

CHAPTER 2
Getting Circled By A Blackhawk.

During the beginning of the pandemic I really dug into some serious shit. A journalist named George Webb was also looking into the theory that the U.S. possibly brought the virus into China. Webb's theory was that a U.S. womens cyclist named Maatje Benassi, who fell ill during the games, was patient zero for the Covid outbreak. George's reporting was a little strange in the way he would tell the story, but he seemed to be one of the only journalists following any leads on the origin of this thing. So I began to dig into his story to see if it had any legs.

I always make a timeline for the characters in my stories, and in this case it was no different. I wanted to see who Maatje was and if she was real, or if she was some sort of undercover government actor. Did she actually have a history, or just appear out of thin air? The timeline I did for Maatje and her husband Matt showed they were both real people, with actual histories, and it showed they were both in the military.

Wanting to join the online fray, I posted an article on April 13th, 2020 entitled "Tracking Matt And Maatje Benassi", where I just showed some of the highlights of their lives, and where they had lived over the years. But I never mentioned where they lived at that time other than the state. Over the next couple of days I shared it with a couple people, including George Webb, who liked the post on Twitter.

A week later George Webb sat down for an interview with CNN's

Donnie O'Sullivan to discuss his patient zero theory, only to be blindsided by the CNN reporter. O'Sullivan asked him how he felt that the Benassi family was living in fear due to his reporting? When Donnie asked George his theory on why on Maatje was patient zero? George fell apart and his answers just didn't make sense. I felt this was some type of a hit job, but from George's answers, I also knew he was really grasping at straws on his theory of Maatje being patient zero.

Not long after the interview I began to hear the sound of a large helicopter flying overhead, so I walked outside to see what was going on. When I got outside the plumbers said this was the copter's third circle. As I looked up I saw a Blackhawk Helicopter about 100 yards above the ground, with a guy with a machine gun hanging out the side looking directly at my building. The plumber said "What the fuck is that for" to which I replied, "I think they are here for me".

Like a flash I went back into my store and deleted the article and thought it was gone forever. I wrote off Webb and his theories, and continued on my own path of research to find out what was really going on with what many were now calling the "plandemic".

My heart was pounding out of my chest. I realized that this was much bigger than writing about Mayor Reid or Starbucks. And I realized the consequences could be very serious, even death.

Just a week later CNN ran the story with Donnie O'Sullivan interviewing George Webb, and I was glued to the screen to see how they played it. At the 25 second mark of the nationally televised CNN interview, they showed an image of the article on my website that I had erased a week prior. This didn't give me the warm and fuzzy feeling, especially after getting flown by what looked like Seal Team Six who were ready to kidnap me.

Not wanting to be kidnapped or killed by the military, I shifted my scopes to Antifa members, or at least what I thought were alleged Antifa members. I figured that the military and government would appreciate some help, but boy was I wrong.

A video surfaced of an individual in Columbus Ohio who was paying younger men to set up tables in the streets during a protest, and many people online were claiming the individual in the video was a man named Aaron Dessner, who is the singer in a band called The National. Aaron has a twin brother named Bryce, who is also in the band, and who also could fit the description of the guy in the video.

They fit the description enough for me to start digging into the brothers to see what I could find that linked them to Antifa. And instead I first found a link between the twin brother's father to Bill Gates, and a conference held in 2012 called Money2020. The twin's father Steven Dessner is the founder and president of Unifund, a company that buys bad debt. But more importantly, he is also the President of Cardlinx, which is a corporation that makes the transfer of digital currency more flexible by obtaining partners who accept their payment systems, where the Senior Director of Microsoft, Neal Bernstein, sits on the Board.

Cardlinx showed a map of the world with countries color coded by their digital currency rating, meaning how much is completely traceable vs. traditional cash currency. The worst countries are coded in red, which include countries such as Mexico and India. The countries that are partially traceable are in yellow, and include countries such as the U.S. and Russia. The countries in green are online with digital currency and are completely traceable, but that only includes one country, China.

The twin's band were playing in Paris on the night of April 15th, 2019, and they were late to their set by roughly 30 minutes. Which I pointed out in the video that I posted to twitter on June 2nd, 2020. I also pointed out that their band was playing only eight minutes from the Notre Dame Cathedral the night the Cathedral burned down, so they could have had time to have set blaze to the Cathedral and still made it to the show.

That was just a small part of the video I made though, the other parts were about me explaining the links between their father and Microsoft, vaccine passports, digital currency, and other subjects that were at that time labeled a conspiracy theory, only to later find out that many of them turned out to be true.

Such as vaccine passports, which is something nobody had ever heard of at the time I posted the controversial video, and which were implemented just a couple months later at restaurants and businesses all across many cities and towns in America, with Philadelphia being one of the most restrictive. I can remember trying to go to Johnny and Brenda's Bar on Girard Avenue, and the person at the door asked us for proof of vaccines for me and my buddy Duke to get in. I quickly let them know that they could go fuck themselves and that I'd never be back. But I was now not just hungry, I was hangry.

Luckily for us pure bloods though, Murph's Bar across the street wasn't acting like Nazis. So we headed over there for not only some cold beers, but also for literally the best Italian food on the East Coast. Shout out to my boy Francesco and Murph's Bar!

I will never forget getting a call from the manager of the twins band Brandon Reid, who was calling me from Ontario in Canada. He was losing his mind on me, saying if I didn't take down the video that I had posted on Twitter right away, that FBI agents would be at my door to arrest me. Of course this caught my attention, so I asked Reid for the contact of the alleged FBI agents he was working with, and he provided me with two names and two phone numbers.

The information Reid provided checked out to be actual FBI agents out of Ohio, which is where the Dessner's are from, and it is also the same State where the "Antifa" guy was paying people to put up picnic benches in the street, who turned out not to be either Dessner.

When I asked Reid about the other portions of my video, such as the connections to Bill Gates and their father, he grew furious and called me every name in the book. Not wanting FBI agents coming to my door, I took down the video and tweeted that I was just threatened by the Dessner's manager, and that I was going to repost the video without the information about the twins.

Just minutes later my Twitter account, which I had since August, 2009, was deleted and my @neojohnbrown account was banned forever. What was off though, was that others claiming that Aaron Dessner was the guy in the video who had thousands of more followers then me, were not banned and the accusatory tweets remained, and still remain. But my account still remains locked and banned till this day. They also banned my boy Duke just for sharing my video, but since the others weren't being banned who were claiming that Aaron Dessner was the "Antifa" guy, I knew that it was the other sections of my video that the FBI was taking issue with.

I was banned forever from the site for a 16 minute video, which we now know per the "Twitter Files" that the censorship was being done at the highest levels of the FBI and other intelligence agencies to hundreds, if not thousands of US Citizens. I used to tell people that I got the Alex Jones treatment, only he was reinstated by Elon Musk in December, 2023 after Musk put up a poll asking if should Alex Jones be allowed back or not, where 70% of the votes were a yes. Journalist Matt Taibbi, who was one of the reporters who broke the Twitter Files, said that the contact between the FBI and Twitter was "constant and pervasive", with Taibbi even claiming that Twitter was a "subsidiary" of the FBI.

Donald Trump tweeted the same video of the man paying the kids to set up tables in the street that I had in my video, with the caption "Anarchists, we see you!". This caused Nathan Caraway, who was the mysterious man in the video to finally come forward. Caraway claimed that he was just trying to help protect people in a CIA, I mean, CNN interview that aired in June, 2020. But CNN didn't ask Caraway any hard questions about the other video that shows him with a large mob hurling rocks at businesses and threatening people with fucking them in the ass if they didn't stand down. Lovely guy, huh?

I kept digging into several theories that I had, but I also began to notice that my Linkedin account was being frequented by someone from the NJ Department Of Child Services, which was clear to me that they were overtly threatening me with the most valuable thing to me in the world, my son. And that was enough for me to put my head down and lay low on the COVID investigations, but soon after I became very sick, so I couldn't investigate anything.

I was hospitalized for a week in May, 2021 with the diagnosis being a diverticulitis flare up, but it wasn't that at all. Over the next two months I literally felt like I was dying, because I was. I couldn't go to the bathroom without excruciating pain, and everything was shutting down, with only a small number of people noticing, or at least letting me know they noticed. Just weeks before my diagnosis my Aunt Debbie looked at me as if she was seeing a ghost. She let me know something was terribly wrong with me, which I tried to just shrug off, but with the awful way that I was feeling, I couldn't.

In July, 2021 I went in for a colonoscopy to try and find the best treatment plan for what I thought was my diverticulitis. Only to learn that my diverticulitis had been misdiagnosed for years as something else. I can remember waking up, still a little groggy and asking the doctor why she looked so disheartened? I jokingly said "did it really look so bad up there?". Her reply struck like lightning. "I am so sorry, but you have cancer."

At that moment it was as if the world suddenly hit a pause button, but the only one paused was me, yet the rest of the world was moving on without me. Even though I was lying down, I felt like I was sinking into the earth. Gravity became twice as strong and a piece of my soul broke off and was deposited into the vast darkness of the universe forever. It felt as if I had been convicted of a crime and was sentenced to death, especially due to the fact that because of COVID restrictions at that time, I was all alone.

They scheduled my surgery for just one week later, which was an extremely dangerous surgery that I didn't even know if I was going to wake up from, and if I did, my chances of surviving looked extremely slim. Over the next week I discussed the songs that I would want to be played at my funeral with my mother, with my first choice being Somewhere Over The Rainbow by that big ass Hawaiian dude, IZ. It was the most heart wrenching conversation of my life.

Since my wife was a stay at home mother at that time, who also doesn't drive, she was going to need help raising our son, Declan. My brothers Sean and Bill came over and both assured me that they would raise my son like he was their own, which I knew they would. While it was relieving to hear, I wanted to live so I could raise him with my beautiful wife, Faridar.

Just a week after my diagnosis I underwent a ten and a half hour surgery where a nearly ten-inch long tumor was removed from my colon. If I did not have the surgery I might have had roughly two months left to live, if that. I was 160 pounds, down from 215, but I was alive.

My tumor became famous after I posted a picture of it on Reddit that got millions of views in just 12 hours. The story of my battle with cancer was also featured in NewsWeek magazine, with a photo of myself right next to Trump and the Pope, which was pretty cool at the time to see for a dying man.

But as I looked out over the city of Camden from my hospital bed, I realized that super villains really do exist, just like the ones in the movies. Camden is a city where billions of dollars are funneled into the pockets of a few. While the city of over 70,000 doesn't even have a grocery store to buy fresh food. It was easy to spot the super villains, but I asked myself, just where were our super heroes?

Camden's the home base of the King of Camden's lair, George Norcross, who has his own helicopter pad atop his taxpayer funded building that he uses so he can swoop in and out of Camden without anyone seeing where he's taking the loot. King George's brother Donald, who was then a NJ State Senator but now he is a U.S Congressman, sponsored a bill that gave $1.6 billion in tax breaks for companies that agreed to make a capital investment in Camden, which is located directly across the Delaware River from downtown Philadelphia.

Camden has been voted the poorest and most dangerous city in the nation numerous times and was in desperate need of jobs for the residents. The city's average long term unemployment rate comes in at just under 15%. Those tax breaks were supposed to be the boost that Camden residents needed, and it was championed by Camden's biggest cheerleader, King George himself, who touted it as a bill that could help save the city.

At least $1.1 billion went to Norcross' own insurance brokerage firm, his business partnerships and charitable affiliations, or clients of the law and lobbying firms of his brother Philip. This distribution of funds was uncovered in an investigation that WNYC and ProPublica did in May, 2019. Even though $1.6 billion was invested in the city, only a handful of menial jobs were created for its residents. Hey, but at least King George got a new building, a building I could literally see from my hospital room for the five days I stayed after my surgery.

Knowing that without modern medical intervention I'd be dead, but also not knowing how much time I had left, I decided to embrace my skill sets in research, journalism, and advocacy, and use those skills to make people believe in justice again. I knew I could find things most people could not, and I knew I could also debate and argue like a Harvard trained attorney. So knowing that 90% of politics is local anyway, I decided to start a campaign of exposing corruption in local governments.

I thought to myself, "what could be a better place to begin the origin story of a new super hero other than their hometown?" And with that thought, the Rabble Rouser began rising.

When I receive a good lead or a response to an OPRA request that has juicy material, I get that same feeling that I did when I was standing in the nurse's office watching the space shuttle explode. I get that uncontrollable urge to want to tell people first, to get the scoop on others who also feel that same urge that I felt as a nine year old growing up in Delran, NJ.

I began by just fishing through social media pages in Delran, and joining all of the groups I could to get ready for the onslaught I had planned. I had my surgery on August 5th, 2021, and I didn't plan on digging in until the new year. That was until I saw a post about a retirement party that was thrown for Delran's local hometown hero, international women's soccer star, Carli Lloyd. Carli was born and raised in Delran before she went on to become a two time Olympic Gold medalist in 2008 and 2012.

Over the years of being involved in looking into local governments, there are two things that when I see, it raises a red flag that most would not notice. The first one that I look out for is more than one politician taking photos for the media while holding shovels with shit eating grins for the groundbreaking of a new building. You can almost be assured that they are either digging up some taxpayers dollars to line their own pockets with or burying some bodies, sometimes literally.

The other thing that I look out for is fireworks, which may seem odd, but it's a great distraction for the masses to pick their pockets while they look at the pretty lights. It's also something that kids love, so the old "It's all for the kids" crap can be played like a trumpet. So when I began to read about the event, and saw that Delran Mayor Gary Catrambone was claiming that this would be "the biggest retirement party ever", I knew the bullshit was deep.

Welcome to what I call, The Delran Debacle.

CHAPTER 3
Fireworks and Shovels

While perusing one of the three FaceBook groups in Delran, I came across a post from a resident who posted a photo of some fireworks with the caption "Your Tax Dollars At Work.". This caught my attention. Little did I know but the night before Delran held a retirement party for women's international soccer superstar, and Delran native, Carli Lloyd. Once I realized the event had fireworks, I knew this could be a way to begin to rouse the town's people.

When I made my first OPRA request to the township and posted my results in the first story you'll see below, I had no idea of the can of worms that I was opening. While some understood that I was simply questioning the costs, many thought I was attacking Carli Lloyd and the need for her to have such an extravagant and expensive party...which I guess was also slightly true. I mean shit, we aren't talking about football here. We were talking about the most boring sport to watch in the world, women's soccer. Just kidding, Mom.

The trolls came after me from all directions, with one main troll leading the way, Queen Trollzilla herself, Wendy Mitchell. In this book we will get into how online trolls like Mitchell use censorship, threats, intimidation, and bullshit consensus to try and make people run away with their tails between their legs. But that shit only makes me stronger. I live for the chaos these trolls try to create to frustrate normal folks enough to just quit. Only I'm not normal, which Trollzilla and her followers soon will learn.

Mitchell was just doing her job though of protecting her political mentor, Delran's Mayor Gary Catrambone AKA DJ Gary Cat, who had surrounded himself with a crew of unquestioning political hacks on Delran's Council. I knew if I was going to get any of the Council members to go against Gary Cat, I'd have to make him toxic politically, and to do so meant a deep dive into the DJ and his business dealings.

Mitchell also blocked me from her Delran 2.0 FaceBook page and asked all of the other moderators to ban me as well. This included a guy who I thought was an old family friend named Mike Garrigues. He obliged Mitchell and banned me from his shitty FaceBook group called "You Know You're From Delran When.". But it should be called "You Know You're From Delran When Mike has told you at least five whoppers", because that Beavis looking goober cannot open his mouth without telling a tall tale. BTW. Fuck you Mike.

Luckily the moderator of the most popular FaceBook group in Delran called Delran Residents Official, Daniel Brennan, hated Mitchell even more than me so he told her to go lick a cat's ass, and allowed me free reign other than one guy that we'll get into later.

Politicians run towards accolades at the same time they run away from trouble, so I knew that if I made Old Gary toxic politically, then at least one of the yes men and women around him would soon turn against him to save their own hide. But what I didn't expect was for Gary Cat himself to attack me first, and even more so, for him to get Carli Lloyd to join in on the attack by posting about me to her nearly two million followers on Facebook. The hate for me at this point was strong by many, but it only made Rabble Rouser more resilient, as ye shall see.

How Much Did Delran Spend on the Lloyd Celebration? 10-15-21

A celebration for a hometown hero was held last night in the small town of Delran. International soccer star, Carli Lloyd, was celebrated with a big event that was put together by the township. Hundreds attended the event, which included a large stage, live music and even a speech by Lloyd that was followed by a massive fireworks display.

Many people in local Delran Facebook groups have questioned the cost of the event. Some have made comments about taxes going up that have been met with a lot of opposition, with other residents saying who cares how much it costs and another person chiming in claiming the fireworks portion was paid for through a donation from a local company...But what's the truth?

For the sake of transparency one would think a local political official would jump in to answer these questions, but just like in most small towns, Delran is not as willingly transparent as one would want...but that's where OPRA requests come in, as I made just this morning to clear up a of few of these questions. Request on opramachine.com

How much did the event cost to put on? At least $37,633.88, which is the cost incurred not including the fire and police hours dedicated to the event. With $12,000 of that being spent on the fireworks to Pyretecnico, $19,500 to Starlite for the stage and entertainment, $2250 to Poznek Enterprises for golf carts, about $2,000 to Robinson Waste for porta potties, and another $1800 for chairs and tents to SSE Party Rentals.

Update: It seems a large portion of the event was covered via donations from local companies, but we are still waiting on exact figures. We are also looking into the fact one of the largest donors possibly has a variance pending before the Township. We will update that info later when it is received.

Delran Mayor Tries To Silence Journalist Looking Into Delran Finances. 10-20-21

It is not everyday as a citizen journalist your hometown mayor tries to silence you, but Wednesday was my lucky day. While scrolling through Delran Mayor Gary Camtrabone's FB page the other day I was shocked to see he had written a completely untrue narrative about a debate I got into on FB regarding the costs regarding the Carli Lloyd retirement event in Delran on the 14th of October, which BTW, I think was a well deserved event.

Let me back up here a bit to give a breakdown of how things got to this point. I belong to a Delran FB group that is quite a lot of fun to watch. I normally do not comment, but after seeing some back and forth regarding the Carli Lloyd retirement event and the costs associated with it, I wanted to help answer some questions. I had no intention of finding possible improprieties, my only intention, originally, was to get the costs associated with the event and publish them. Which I did in this article.

Once the article hit the two Delran pages where I posted, it got hundreds of hits in just the first hour. The comments started coming in, with many people seeming angry that I would do such a thing as question a local government with a multi-million dollar budget that spends their tax money, and others in support of my investigation. Many said that they don't care what the costs were, that the kids' smiles made up for it all. With others saying it didn't cost enough.

There was a third group of people though who were claiming that the $37,633 number I received directly from the Delran Clerk didn't include the offsets from the donations made by the donors, with one donor claiming they paid directly for the fireworks, which cost $12,000. At this point, I felt the best thing to do would be to reach back out to the clerk to get a list of all donations that were made towards the event so I could help clear up the question of how much of the 37k was offset by donations.

In record time the Clerk returned a financial breakdown of monies in and monies out, yet the monies out didn't match the numbers from the prior chart. Since the lists did include donations, including the $12,000 from the fireworks donor, I posted the list on the two Delran pages for people to see the info that I was given, but since I knew it didn't match, I requested a clarification from the clerk, this is where it got really strange.

The Clerk responded "The $37,633.88 in expenses from the first report provided were paid by the Township from the Recreation: Special Programs budget and were not offset by donations. I have attached another copy of the report.". As you can see, that is quite a different response from the prior one that listed almost $35,000 in donations. So I went back again for clarity and received a third set of numbers that also didn't match the other two, and also didn't include the $12,000 expense for the fireworks. So I'm like WTF?

During the sharing of these numbers with the one Delran group that didn't ban me, Delran Residents Official, a post was made where a donor that tagged and named me in the first two words and went on to claim that I "dragged her family and business name through the mud", which was and is completely untrue. This post was piled on by dozens of people calling me all kinds of nasty names and questioning my integrity. One Nurse from Lourdes Hospital even checked my page and found out I had cancer and made a post telling me that it is because of my Karma. Now that's a great bedside manner right there.

Beep beep, my phone alerts me of a new post. It's the Delran Mayor Gary Camtrabone slinging accusations about a non-resident defaming a resident and a donor to the Carli Lloyd event, but he didn't directly name me. The Mayor shared it on his and the townships pages. That's when my phone began to ring. "Yo Dude, what the hell is going on, is the Mayor talking about you?". It was a lovely day yesterday, dealing with cancer doctors and defending my name because I printed what the Delran clerk wrote.

What would make the Mayor of Delran want to attack me and try to have me end my investigation? I am a citizen journalist who just wanted to know how much an event costs so I could share it with people who were arguing over air without any real numbers to reach a conclusion from. The Mayor could have taken the opportunity in his post to clarify the discrepancies in the accounting, but he didn't. That was what all the debate was about, not the variance that he mentioned, yet the mayor decided to use his position of authority to throw a variance seeker under the bus, why?

One thing is clear, the Mayor of Delran is trying to use his position of power to silence the media from investigating an issue of public concern, and that, Mr. Mayor, is illegal. If I were the donor seeking a variance, I'd also be seeking an attorney. If I were a Delran resident seeking transparency, I'd be seeking a new Mayor.

Delran Brings On New Deputy Clerk As Financial Records Controversy Heats Up. 10-25-21

Tomorrow night at 7 pm the Delran Town Council will be having their first public meeting since a controversy that has embroiled the town regarding the financial records for the Carli Lloyd retirement celebration that was held on October 14th. The controversy stems from several OPRA requests made by myself seeking the costs associated with the event, which one would think should have been easy to do, yet it has not been for Delran's Clerk, Jamey Eggers.

Eggers has provided several conflicting answers regarding the costs and donations of the event, answers that once provided to the public, have only left more questions. Eggers claimed that none of the more than $35,000 in donations that were made by the donors offset the costs that she had previously supplied on a spreadsheet, a claim that once published sent the town of Delran into what has become an extremely heated controversy, with Eggers right in the middle of it.

When the online controversy heated up due to the conflicting responses by Eggers, Delran's Mayor Gary Catrambone decided to make a public announcement regarding the controversy. Instead of explaining the questions regarding the conflicting responses made by Eggers, Catrambone's statement shifted the focus to a variance for a Sports Complex being sought by one of the donors who we still don't know where their money went that was meant for the event. In his statement, the Mayor asserted that a nonresident (me), made claims of coercion and bribery regarding the variance being sought by the donors, which I never asserted and is completely untrue. A hearing for that variance was canceled last week and has been put on hold until further notice.

That notice will likely be approved by Delran's own covert Communication Director and Administrator of the Delran Residents 2.0 FB group, Wendy Mitchell. Mitchell, who is also not a Delran resident, has been the Admin of the popular Delran Residents 2.0 FB group since 2017. In March of this year Delran hired the Delran Residents 2.0 page moderator as the towns Communication's Manager for $36,000 per year, a position that creates a direct conflict of interest and one that cannot be located on any of the townships online directories. It is reported that Mitchell rules the 2.0 page with an iron fist, blocking and banning any Delran Dissenter, such as me. Mitchell was even caught colluding to silence me with another popular Delran page moderator, Mike Garrigues, in a plan to stop my dissent against Delran.

Dissent is not just controlled and censored on the Delran Residents 2.0 page, where Mitchell had the right to do so, but it's being done on the Township and the Mayor's public pages as well, which is not legal to do so. If the township would censor all comments, that's one thing, but they cherry pick the positive ones and block any negative ones, which according to the NJ ACLU, is not legal.

Now that it is known that Mitchell is both a paid employee of Delran in her job is the Communications Director, the legal question will soon be asked of a Judge whether or not the 2.0 page must considered a public page and be open to the public since Mitchell is obviously communicating on behalf of the township from the 2.0 FB page.

As Delran gets ready for its first public council meeting since the controversy broke, Eggers is most likely breathing a slight sigh of relief as Delran prepares to bring on Melissa Larkin with Eggers to assist her as Deputy Clerk. Hopefully Delran citizens will get the answers they deserve from the Mayor and the town's new Director of Communications tomorrow night regarding the controversy surrounding the donations for Carli's retirement, otherwise the Mayor might have his own retirement party, as he exits stage left.

Transcript/Minutes From October 26th, 2021 Delran Council Meeting.

Mayor Gary Catrambone: (Mr. Catrambone) reported that on October 14th, the Township hosted a tremendous event to celebrate Carli Lloyd. After being separated through the pandemic it was great to be able to hold the event outside and safely. He believes this is exactly what the residents wanted and especially what the children needed. Carli Lloyd is the epitome of hard work and the relentless pursuit of self-improvement. Her speech at the event was wonderful and each and every member of the Delran community has been inspired to be better versions of themselves because of Carli. We received tremendous support for the event from the volunteers to the corporate sponsors. Although not everything is in yet, it looks like 51% of the total cost of the event was offset by corporate sponsors and donations. The Philadelphia Eagles were nice enough to provide video footage for the evening which will be available soon. Delran Township Public Works did a stellar job as always. Mr. Catrambone thanked the Delran Police Department, Delran Fire Department, Delran EMS, Riverside Fire Department, Cinnaminson Fire Department, Burlington County Fire Department, Burlington County Sheriff's Office and the NJ State Police. It was a tremendous undertaking and planned in a much shorter time frame.

Councilman Lynn Jeney (Mr. Jeney) echoed the comments from the Mayor regarding the Carli Lloyd celebration. It was exceptional for the Township but what is more impressive is the guidance, leadership and example Carli showed to the children in attendance.

Councilman Tyler Burrell (Mr. Burrell) stated that it is great to see the large group in attendance tonight. He reminded residents that if you would like to speak, please raise your hand and be recognized and approach the front. Please state your name and address for the record. All remarks should be addressed to the Council President and each speaker will be allotted five minutes. All statements are part of the public record.

Patrick Duff (Transcript): Hey, how are you doing? My name is Patrick Duff. I'm actually a Haddon Heights resident. I grew up right here at 812 Chester Avenue. My brother was the first heavyweight state champion in wrestling. My family won six state championships all together in football, wrestling, and track. So to be called a non-resident from Delran, is a little frustrating.

Burrell: Well, we welcome you back.

Duff: I'm glad to be back. Just so you know what I do. I'm a researcher, a writer and an activist. So I go all around to towns, all around New Jersey seeking open public records requests. Just last year I sued six municipalities and I won every single lawsuit. Okay? So when I file it against Delran, I can be sure that number seven is in my pocket.

And I'll tell you why. Because Delran is censoring comments on your Facebook page, on a public page. If you just look up, just type in "social media", "aclu new jersey", and "public comments". You'll see very easily that the case law states that you cannot censor comments. You have to be content neutral. Meaning you can't just allow the positive ones, and take away the negative ones, that's not the way it works. Okay?

Now, what I also find actually appalling, is that in a move that I think was a move to try to help silence any dissent in Delran, the Township took on a communications director earlier this year that runs one of the Township's Facebook pages that censors comments on there also. Which is a major conflict of interest.

Now I don't know if anybody knows, you're talking about Carly Lloyd? Carli Lloyd has almost 2 million people on her fan page. Do you know whose name she put on her fan page, telling me to stop questioning the finances into the event? Me! Do you know how many hate messages I got in my inbox because of that?

The Mayor put me on his FaceBook page too, calling me a non-resident. Saying I'm questioning things, saying I'm claiming that coercion is happening and all these things with variance.

Which was never claimed. I'm very careful with what I do. I'm very careful to stick by the facts. So my lawyer can prepare a lawsuit to sue you, and have you open up the Facebook comments, and make the Delran 2.0 page either open to the public, because it's being run by a public employee. Or have the person that's a public employee give up their admin status to it, because it doesn't make any sense. But it does make sense if you're in a communist country to limit the comments. But not in democracy.

We live in a democracy where people need to have a voice. When you silence their voice, people get frustrated, and they get scared. I've gotten more private messages from people scared to talk in Delran than any town that I've ever worked in doing this open public records information stuff. Okay? Literally, okay?

I don't know if you've seen it, but Martin Luther King, his first civil rights battle happened in Maple Shade, New Jersey. He was living in Camden, New Jersey. I'm the researcher that brought that to light. I found things that no other researcher in the world has found out about Martin Luther King.

I'm a high school dropout in Delran, by the way. All right? So I take these things personally, because I was really forgotten about in school. They put me in a closet, because I asked questions in Delran. I told people Columbus didn't discover anything, and they put me in the closet. Now look, everybody agrees now, everybody agrees that Columbus didn't discover anything.

So I want an apology from the Mayor. A public apology from the Mayor for placing me on his Facebook page and calling me a non-resident. Saying things I didn't do that then put Carli into a position of putting me on her Facebook page with millions of people. The "non-resident", well she's a non-resident too!

So I'm asking two things, open your Facebook page up for comments. Don't close all your comments, Let your citizens comment. The negative comments make you better as public officials. That's the way it works.

And number two, either take Wendy down from the 2.0 page as your employee, or fire her! Or, open that page up to the public like the judge will probably wind up making you do anyway. So I'm seeking a public apology, Mayor. I really think you owe me one.

Burrell: Great thank you very much uh for your statement uh your comment this evening uh seriously great work with the uh Martin Luther King discovering that that's uh fantastic news um but in in addressing your your two items that you brought up to us um we're not a position to comment on any uh litigation as you just mentioned. Um there's no comment on any pending litigation I'm sure you can respect that pending litigation.

Duff: There's no pending litigation. I'm asking you guys not to make the pending litigation, so we can make it fair for your citizens.

Burrell: Um, second there was uh, you know, I'll hand it over to the Mayor. If you, Mayor, want to address the administrative issues regarding um, your Facebook page. He is referring to your Facebook page and the admin issue regarding the communications director who is also personnel. So if you would like to comment.

Mayor Catrambone: No. The Delran Township Facebook page is, I'm sure, within compliance.

Burrell: Any other questions from members of the public or comments

Duff: I should say I actually just wanted to finish my comment.

Burrell: You're more than welcome to. You have to come up to the podium. Thank you.

Duff: The reason why I started this all in Delran by the way, is because there was just a simple question on the FaceBook pages of how much did the event cost, right? So I got back the event costs. That was the first OPRA I got, it said $37,633.88. It said that was all the event costs, part of it was for the fireworks. I put that up on the FaceBook page, and people started going nuts, saying there's donations that help pay for all this stuff.

So I put in another OPRA request saying I want to know the donations, and I got a request back with different numbers that didn't add up from the original request, and it showed about thirty five thousand dollars in donations. Okay? The third request I made was to clarify how much, and this is specific, so everybody understands. How much of the donations offset the costs of the event? Jamie Eggers replied to me that "none of the cost of the event was offset by donations".

When I released that information to the Delran public, let's just say the poop hit the fan. Okay? I think that the information, and the lack of clarity, which should have been given in the Mayor's post, not to step on the variance holders neck, the lack of clarity has caused the Township to feel like there's been something hidden. It definitely makes me feel like there is. Now the Mayor said that 51% of the costs were covered by donations? Well that wasn't given to me in my OPRA request when I requested it. They just said all the costs were 37,000 dollars, and that none of those costs were offset by donations. But now everything's changing?

I would request that when you get a simple OPRA request for figures for an event, which should be really easy to do. When they're not, that's when people start asking questions. So you can go look through the OPRA requests and see what was said, and please, please clarify those numbers.

Burrell: Yeah, gotcha. So, so, for the record, um everything, all our financials, the good thing about municipal government is the most regulated industry I've ever worked in, for sure. We have auditors. We have CFOs. We have administrators. Purchase orders, everything is well documented down to the penny. And your OPRA request came in early in the process. The figures haven't changed um, if they are changing it's because more purchase orders are finally getting cut. The billing process is not like private business, where it comes in and the CFO writes the check right away. We have processes here. But I do want to clarify the allegation that the money was not offset or was put into this bank account that nobody's aware of. According to state law there's for us to accept donations there's a process which is called a dedication by rider. Uh, statute 40a 4-39 for anyone who's interested in reading about it. We did this actually in 2018. We dedicated an account called Delran Events. Um Delran Events, which was dedicated by rider. It's approved by uh, it's the Director of the New Jersey Department of Community Affairs. That's where all donations for any events that come into this Township go into that account. It's called the Delran events fund, which is actually a trust account. All those donations that came into this event, 40 or 38 plus thousand, whatever the number may be, went into that account. When bills are purchased, when anything is purchased, whether it's fireworks, porta potties or if it's cable costs for the event, they get put out of the RAC budget. It doesn't get itemized out of that trust account, yet. So it's technically not an offset in that, that the check itself from a donor who paid for the fireworks, or paid for the tabletop, but in the end it all nets out for the same amount. Right? If you have a bank account and there's a hundred dollars in there, and you spend a hundred dollars, but you later put 100 back in. You still got 100 in there. So it is offsetting at the end when it all balances out so that all is crystal clear there.

Round 2

Burrell: (speaking to the Mayor) Want to get to this statement? Would you like to give the figures?

Mayor Catrambone: I did. Didn't I?

Burrell: No. Please go ahead.

Mayor Catrambone: Sure, so the folks that were asking about the numbers for the Carli Lloyd event, these are the the expenses as we believe are complete, except for those line items that would be police overtime and public works over time, as they are not from the budget item list that we have, and that is calculated separately. Although I do remind you that all the other services that came to help us, like the sheriff's department, were paid by their respective organizations. So the total for this was $90,456.93 and the total donations were $46,166, of which seven thousand have not as yet been received but have been committed as recently as today, to make sure that they were on their way. so that's 51 percent of the total budget for the event. It came from this, the RAC's budget, as well as the special events trust, as well as the donations, left us I think with the uh, several thousand dollar uh, remainder uh, that will be put toward the next event and will be fine. We continue to request additional sponsorships for the future events that come up. So those are the numbers and as we said half of that 51 was paid by private and corporate donations.

Burrell: Great. Thank you. Any other public comments at this time? Just wrap this up and yeah very quickly

Duff: I just want to say, it's kind of upsetting, what the Mayor just said.

Burrell: Mr. Duff if you could just wrap this thing up, I appreciate it.

Duff: Thank you. The OPRA request said $37,000 in costs. Not $90,000 in costs. So I don't know where these extra costs come from? Now there's 40 something thousand dollars in donations, when it only showed 30 something thousand. So the numbers changed, and it shouldn't be changing. That's all I want to say. Thank you very much. If it were to change in my business my manager would be fired right away.

Carli Lloyd Retirement Party Cost

Delran $666 Per Minute! 10-31-21

Who would have thought that a retirement party for a hometown hero such as Carli Lloyd, could also mean the possible political retirement of the Delran Mayor, and or the Council President, but it just might. The 2.5 hour retirement party for Carli Lloyd was planned under the watchful eye of Mayor Gary Catrambone and the Recreation Advisory Committee, who when all is said and done, spent over $100,000 on the party, with a portion being offset, or not, by some questionable donations.

More questions were raised when it was learned that Delran hired a moderator of a popular FB group called Delran Residents 2.0, Wendy Mitchell, who has been censoring the Townships public pages like the old German Kaiser Himself as well as the 2.0 page of any negative comments or posts about the Town government. Mayor Camtrabone claimed that the censorship was completely compliant, but that's not what the current court precedents nor the ACLU say.

Now even more questions have arisen since we learned the Council President publicly claimed that the town received three bids for the two resolutions passed to spend $61,500 for a stage and video screens, yet in the information sent to us from the town in our OPRA requests, it only shows they received 2 bids. They also did not pass resolutions for any of the other $29,000 in contracted costs for the event.

The Chairmen of the Recreation Advisory Committee, 21 year old Colin Rafferty, made a claim on FB that the contract for the stage said the balance was to be paid "post event", but it did not say such a thing. When I pointed out to Colin that the contract did not say what he claimed, he got silent. The contract said the balance was due on 10/14/21, which was the day of the event, and not "post event", as Colin claimed. The only reason Colin is claiming that the payment was to be accepted post event, is to try and explain why the town lied about the total costs being only $37 633.88 in their responses in the original OPRA requests, when we later found out they were $90,456, plus the police and public works costs they will have spent well over 100k!

We now wait anxiously for the elected and selected officials, or possibly their Mothers, to answer to the public. Whether they will or not is left to be unanswered, but when Colin Rafferty was questioned about the contract language, he did not answer. No, instead of the guy in control of helping spend $100,000 of taxpayers money explaining himself, his Mother jumped in and wrote "This guy better back off my Son", in an attempt to protect her baby.

Well Mom, your baby is making big boy decisions now. If he cannot answer for himself, maybe he should think of a new career, because politics is not for the faint of heart and sometimes demands tough answers to tough questions, and not from his Mom.

CHAPTER 4
Duff Deposes Delran

One Christmas while I was at my Grandfather's house with my family, I managed to get into a heated political debate with my brother Sean. Even though I cannot remember what the argument was over, I can remember my Uncle Hal pulling me aside to discuss the post debate results. My Uncle Hal Bozarth was one of the most powerful lobbyists in the state of NJ. When he passed a couple of years ago, his funeral was attended by the most powerful people in the state of NJ, including past and present Governors, Senators, Congresspeople and the heads of the corporations that pay the salaries of all the lobbyists on State Street. So I would say he knew a little something about negotiations and debate.

When he pulled me aside, he first buttered me up a bit by telling me I had won the argument. But then he paused to take a long drag of his cigarette. Upon exhaling he looked up to the sky and slowly said "technically, but nobody listened". Which felt like a gut shot. He then went on to tell me that since we were both heated and talking over each other, that nobody actually heard what either of us were saying, especially my brother Sean or me, so our points were wasted.

He told me that I should take the opportunity to be quiet and listen until the other person has finished their point. Once they are finished I should confirm they are finished, and after I get confirmation say "you know what, I really never thought of it that way. You could be right, but did you ever think about it like this?". Which allows for your opponent to drop their guard, and more importantly, it gives you the chance to actually make your own points without an argument ensuing.

My Father is proud to say that he didn't raise any pussies, and I am not talking about the fact that he didn't have any daughters. As a kid a conversation where we attempted to evade him in any way, was immediately met with "Oh, Bullshit". My friends were scared to call my house for fear that my Dad would answer. They would just hang up after the first few times that they'd called and he answered, because otherwise he'd interrogate them if they ever asked for me. One night when my brothers and I decided to not come down for dinner after being called several times just so we could keep playing our Nintendo. My Dad wasn't having it. He warned us one more time before he came upstairs and smashed the Nintendo under his foot, and just said, "Dinner".

As a young teenager I would often say "you know what I mean", to finish a thought while talking to my Mother. While I thought this was OK, my Mom would say "No, I don't know what you mean. Please explain?". It pissed me off at first, but I soon realized that it would just be better to explain myself than to, "you know what I mean", my Mother. When I was around six or seven I stole a piece of bazooka bubble gum from the 7-11 in Delran, the same one that's still there on Haines Mill Road today. When I got into my mother's car I felt like I had gotten away with it, only when my mother saw the gum that I had stolen she became furious. She made me go back in and either give it back or pay for it if they didn't want to take it back, and most importantly, she made me apologize for being wrong.

I really cannot stand the feeling of being wrong, it's actually quite terrible, but some are capable of learning to live with it. Some of the strongest human emotions we have are shame and embarrassment. It's what gives humans our moral compass. It shapes what we find to be acceptable or not. And has been around well before any religion or cultural norms to give us our internal map to intrinsically know what is right from wrong. Some people are narcissists though, and these people would rather die than admit they are wrong or apologize, which is something I believe Mayor Catrambone is infected with. I tell my son and his friends that if they just tell the truth about something they did wrong, mistake or not, it diffuses the situation and that feeling of being a loser ends upon admission.

Delran officials knew that they were wrong in how they handled the situation on every level so far, but their refusal to admit it only drove me to dig more. If the Mayor had just apologized and admitted that the way the numbers were given to me in the OPRA requests were convoluted, and said sorry about the message where he claimed I said bribery and coercion took place regarding a variance holder, the issue of the Carli party would have most likely disappeared. But instead he doubled down and acted like I was at fault for simply questioning him, which only caused me to dig into DJ Gary Cat and his shady business dealings involving his family members even more.

The art of cross examination is something that I have become extremely proficient at over the years. It is one of our most valuable constitutional rights that we have available to us. The keys to the art are people's prior statements and facts you can enter into the record, and more importantly, how the two are at odds with the answers of those you are deposing at that time. Once you know where the contradictions exist, you know what questions to ask.

Now that I knew the Township was hiding the real costs of the event, and that the Mayor lied publicly about me by claiming I alleged bribery and coercion took place regarding a donor to the Carli Party, when I did not. I knew where I would begin my series of cross examinations of the Delran officials. The answers to the OPRA requests, past videos of council meetings, and publicly made statements act as my discovery. I use them to build a timeline for the person that I am questioning to find any contradictions in the answers that they are giving. Once they answer my leading questions in the affirmative, they know that they are admitting to their own wrong doing, so instead they start dancing like Michael Jackson in a room full of young boys. Oops, sorry, that wasn't dancing.

Cross examination is like leading the witness down a path where people are hiding behind trees with bats, but not all of the trees have people behind them. If they answer the question wrong, they get whacked with the bat of the prior statement or fact, which you then enter into the record as evidence of the contradiction. After a couple of times getting hit with a Louisville of truth, the witness doesn't know which tree has the person with the bat standing behind it anymore or not. So they begin to try and evade all of the trees by not answering your questions. Which only chops away at their own credibility in the eyes of the jurors, or the public, until the witness is impeached, or even better, finally breaks.

At this point I was lining up the Delran Officials for a walk down a treacherous path of their own contradictions. I have to give Burrell and Catrambone credit though, because those two took a licking and kept on ticking, or in this case, talking, which is exactly what I wanted them to do. As they keep talking they get lost amongst the trees, dazed and confused by all of the mental whacks to their own conscience until that most wonderful moment, that moment that every attorney and jury waits for. That moment where the witness finally breaks and says "You want the truth? The truth? I'll give you the truth. You're Goddamn right I ordered that code red", and the judge orders the witness taken into custody.

While I couldn't have Delran officials taken into custody, I could convict them in the most important court of all, the court of public opinion.

DJ Mayor Spins a Web of Corruption. 11-2-21

The Township of Delran has been quite lively over the last couple of weeks due to some controversy surrounding the costs of the Carli Lloyd retirement event and my investigations into those costs. I have become quite notorious in the town and surrounding areas due to this, with some even making memes of my beautiful face, and others cheering me on like I am Rudy sacking the QB. In this case that QB is Delran's Mayor Gary Catrambone, who as you will see made some very questionable play calls that could land him on a bench in court.

Gary Catrambone works with Frank Catrambone at Center Stage Entertainment, which is located at 902 West Laurel Road in Lindenwold, NJ. Center Stage Entertainment provides DJ, photo booths and lighting services. These are similar services to the ones provided for the Carli Lloyd event that a company called Go Events was contracted by the town to do. Go Events Inc was paid a total of $5950 to provide a DJ and a band for two and a half hours. Now since Gary is a part of Center Stage Entertainment, one would wonder why he just didn't hire his own company to provide the DJ and the band, I mean, that's what the guy does, right? But as anyone in politics knows that is a big no no...one of the biggest.

An elected official cannot award contracts to his own company or that of his family and or co-workers. This is done to avoid schemes like inflated costs that directly hinder the services needed for the communities to thrive instead of one individual and their family and friends. Services that are now desperately needed for the residents on Stewart Ave who experienced the worst flooding they have seen in decades.

If I were speaking live on stage right now I'd ask DJ Catrambone to play a drum roll, but I think they'd turn the music up real loud so you couldn't hear what I am about to say.

Go Events was registered on November 18th of 2020 in the State of Nevada, yet they bare a NJ address on their registration, a NJ address that just so happens to be the same address for Center Stage Entertainment, and also just happens to be registered to the Mayor's Nephew, Frank Catrambone.

WTF? I think the record just skipped.

Transcripts From November 9th, 2021 Delran Council Meeting.

Tyler Burrell: just for the record your name and address please

Patrick Duff, I'm a Haddon Heights resident rather not state the address because I've actually had threats...

Tyler Burrell: That's fine, that's fine...

Patrick Duff: I've actually had physical threats against me. Somebody told me they're going to shoot me if I didn't stay offline for trying to do an investigation into the finances of the Carli LLoyd event. Isn't that wonderful, isn't that a real nice thing? I called the Burlington County Sheriff and they're now investigating it. People wonder why I'm doing this? Why are you investigating this town and looking into this town? First let me tell you that 14 weeks ago I found out I had cancer. For the last four years I thought I had diverticulitis, but 14 weeks ago I found out I had cancer. I found out that it had a perforation in it, and it was leaking in my body. It was killing me, I was dying. I was about two months away from dying, from being dead. This perforated tumor that was in my body was sitting there in my body basically killing me for years, and nobody knew it, because nobody looked, and that's what I'm doing. I am taking a look at your finances to see where these go. If there's a tumor that needs to be removed from your town, and I can tell you that the tumor that was removed from me was 10 inches long just 13 weeks ago. I'm alive today because they did it. Thank God! I thank God every day that I can see my son. But I want to leave this world a better place for him, in case I cannot make it past the next couple weeks!

And the only way to do that is with honest representation for my son. so I chose to pick Delran, just to look at a simple financial record of the carly lloyd event. It should have been a really easy thing. You should have sent me the financials, all the PO's were already cut. Mayor, you said nothing illegal happened. I can tell you that I have proof that there's contracts that show the video services, and the stage services were split purposefully to avoid getting bids. That's illegal.

I can show that your company, Center stage Entertainment, actually solicited quotes from these companies, and that somebody from your company signed for Go Events that are owned by one of your relatives and your co-worker. That's not legal, sir. To say it's to say it's legal. Could you explain to me then, why you didn't just hire Center Stage Entertainment to do all these events? You had to go around and hire this Go Events company that you can't even figure out who they are, because they're registered in Nevada. It took me a little while, but I found them. So let's just be honest here, the slow perforation of a cancerous tumor in my body was killing me.

But the slow perforation of the finances in Delran are making it so the tax structure in this town is unbearable for the citizens. The people on Stewart Ave, they didn't get checks to help them with the clean out of their basement. They got a firefighter showing up, and they're volunteers working their butts off to try and help people. But I can tell you this, that me looking into this is just another town that I've done.

I've done Point Pleasant Beach, Philadelphia. I've done the police system in Philadelphia. I actually changed the 9-1-1 system after the 9-1-1 calls were made in Philadelphia at Starbucks.

They changed the 911 system because of research I did. So listen, I don't know if it's a one-time thing, Mayor, but you did hire somebody from your company, you did hire your family member. You're the head of the Recreation Committee, you're the one that signs off, there's no way you can say you didn't know. There's no way that Jeff Hatcher can say he didn't know that Go Events was being signed for by Alex Glover, who's an employee of Center Stage Entertainment.

That's on your financial disclosure, that that's where you work. Man that's, listen, come clean. Be real. The citizens of your town are not asking that you step down, and I'm not asking you to step down. But be real. You insulted me. You said I defamed people. You said that I claimed that there's coercion and bribery. I never did that. I never said anything bad about Carli, I never said anything bad about the celebration. I simply asked questions of the finances, and was given different answers. Then that was put in a public forum, and you said something that I did that I didn't do.

And as I said, 13 weeks ago I had cancer extracted from my body. I was dying. I have stage two high risk cancer, and they want me to do six months of chemotherapy now. I could die next month. I don't want to leave the world worse for my son. So if the question is, why am I doing this? That's it. But please answer the question of why did you hire somebody from your company that's your own relative, and somebody you work with? Which you know is not legal to contract with. And why did you avoid Tyler, why did you avoid getting RFP's on bids that are greater than the $44,000 threshold that you know you have to get bids on? I can prove that you did, because I have contracts that show that both services are included. People in this town are sending me stuff left and right. So I have them already. So admit it. You bid split and you handed contracts to your friends. thank you very much

Mayor Ctrambone: Thank you for your comments Mr Duff.

Tyler Burrell: With regards to the uh, bid splitting uh Sal, Sal was involved. Sal is our Solicitor who was involved in the process and consulted throughout that. Sal, was that process up to your snuff?

Sal: There was no bid splitting.

Tyler Burrell: Thank you Solicitor.

Round 2
Tyler Burrell: Mr Duff, we really only recognize people once.

Patrick Duff: You just recognized him twice.

Burrell: I know.

Duff: Just pointing that out for the record. I got to ask you, Tyler, did the Township receive any quotes that were above $44,000 that included the video service along with the staging services?

Burrell: Can you say that one more time please?

Duff: Did the Township receive any quotes that were above $44,000 that you would have had to seek an RFP for? Did the Township receive any quotes or the consultants receive any quotes that included all of these services that were above $44,001 with the video services and the stage services? You've got to answer this carefully, Tyler.

Burrell: I'm well aware of what you are trying to do.

Duff: I'm asking you a question.

Burrell: If you would give me the opportunity to answer I'd be more than happy to. So, Sal was a part of the process the whole time, Sal is our Solicitor, everyone who was involved with the event consulted with Sal. The bid splitting that you claim. There are proposals earlier on that include from other vendors that are extremely high, right? As we were working on the event the

RAC...

Duff: Do you mind stating the vendors?

Burrell: The vendors are all the ones that we have, uh, Starlite, Spellcasters. There's a couple of them, but I don't have all of them with me. I know there is an OPRA request for them.

Duff: But you do have quotes that are above the $44,000 threshold. Is that correct?

Burrell: No, those are proposals, those are concept proposals. But let me explain what you are talking about the bid threshold level, and Sal can, can, put this in maybe layman's terms. At, at the, at the point where we made decisions, the you, uh, the resolutions, right? The non-fair and open contracts, right? That we passed.

Duff: Two separate ones. Correct?

Burrell: Yes, there were two separate ones for that, right?

Duff: For the same event. Correct?

Burrell: Yeah, it's the same event. They're two different services. For the video service, if you would let me explain I'd be able to do that, thank you. So for the video service we attempted to get three quotes. Ok, there was a quote from..uh you have to bear with me. Kathrina or something like that.

Duff: Kathedral?

Burrell: Yes, Kathedral, and there was Waltronics.

Duff: BTW Kathedral doesn't do video. I'm just letting you know. The quote was split for Spellcaster.

Burrell: All right Mr. Duff. You are going to have to sit down.

Sal: What is your question?

Duff: Yeah, My question is did you receive any quotes above the $44,000 threshold? Yes or no?

Sal: It is not a yes or no question.

Duff: He's placating.

Burrell: Mr. Duff if you'll please be seated and I'll answer, I'll be more than happy to answer the question.

Sal: You've interrupted him now three times. Could you allow him...your question has been answered. It's been duly noted on the record. It's been filmed by video, your friend is filming me right now. Allow the gentlemen to answer the question. Are you capable of doing that?

Duff: It's a yes or no question.

Sal: No it's not. No no no no....

Duff: Did the township receive bids above $44,000? That's a yes or no question.

Sal: No it's not.

Duff: OK, I have the bids.

Sal: You are making factual assumptions which are incorrect. Mr. Tyler had attempted to answer your question. It's not to your satisfaction because it doesn't fit your narrative.

Duff: Real quick. There were original bids that were above $44,000.

Sal: No one has said that.

Duff: That the same company literally split the bid, isn't that right?

Sal: No sir Mr. Duff, no one has made that statement. You have made that statement because it fits your narrative.

Duff: I have proof.

Sal: No one has made that statement. Thank you. Mr Burrell, I I I, I think...

Burrell: I'll finish my statement and then we will move on. Umm, there was, so for the video there was, uh, we attempted to get three quotes, right? Three quotes, one company could not meet the specs and sent a letter that meets the standards of the law. Uh, as advised by the solicitor. Then with respect to the stage slash sound, there were three quotes attempted to be get for that. We went with the lowest most responsible bidder in conjunction with Sal's counsel. Uh, a non fair and open contract, and then we met the election requirement to disclose if there were any political contributions. That is the extent of how we got to that contract in question.

Duff: But there were contracts above that amount, Correct?

Sal: NO, no sir, there was no...

Duff: There were no quotes above that amount?

Sal: Sir, no one is making that statement. You are making it. Your question is assuming a fact that is not true.

Duff: So Sal, I am just asking a question.

Sal: (Heated) My Name is not Sal! My name is Mr. Siciliano and you'll address me as such. I am the Township Solicitor. We are not on a first name basis.

Duff: I appreciate that.

Sal: I don't address you as Patrick. I address you as Mr. Duff.

Duff: I really appreciate the attitude but I'm asking a question. You are a public representative.

Sal: Yes sir I am.

Duff: Well you owe the public an answer. So don't talk to me like you got an attitude. OK?

Sal: You can be quiet Sir.

Duff: (Heated) You're a public representative buddy. (Audience clapping) You answer the question.

Sal: Your question is..

Duff: Did you receive any quotes above the $44,000 for all services, is the question? Yes or no.

Sal: It's not a yes or no.

Duff: Thank you very much.

Sal: It's not or yes or no. It's not a yes or no question.

CHAPTER 5
The Receipts

OPRA (Open Public Records Act) is NJ's version of the Freedom Of Information Act. It allows you to ask for all types of records from government entities, including emails, texts, settlement agreements, police records and all types of different documents. In New Jersey we are blessed to have www.opramachine.com, which was invented by Gavin Rozzi, and allows users to easily make requests through their database of hundreds of NJ government entities. I'll be honest here, Gavin is like Santa to me, because I feel like a child on Christmas morning every time I get an email from the Opramachine to open.

The most important aspect of what I do consists of OPRA requests and finding moles inside of the municipal buildings, or at least making those I am investigating think that I have a mole. The art of misdirection is a very powerful tool. Getting your adversaries thinking about who is feeding you information is key to starting to tear the inner circle of your foes into little pieces. Even if you have no mole, make them believe that you do even if you found your information elsewhere.

While Gary Cat and his band of merry political hacks thought that I had a mole inside the Township at this point, because I knew about the other contracts above $44,000 that had not been provided to me. No mole actually existed, I had merely called a vendor that lost the bid who not only provided me with the bids that he sent to the Township, but he also let me know that the Township directly requested that he split the contracts.

Confirming my suspicions regarding the Township bid splitting. There was also chatter online of a $150,000 contract from Starlite that the Township originally was going to go with, but the Mayor denied its existence at a council meeting just weeks prior to the Carli Party, but I had a source telling me otherwise.

When engaging in political rabble rousing, it's always good to find other issues that make your adversaries look bad and highlight them for the public to see, as you will see I did with the Delran's contract for trash collection. This way you keep the public's interest in your plight, which if you present the stories correctly, becomes their plight as well. You will see that other people begin to join the fight, some from behind the scenes, some vocal online in FaceBook groups, and others vocal at council meetings. But just like Tom Sawyer painting that fence, others are bound to join.

Politics must be played as a long game, so it's best to constantly push for new information that can affirm, or reaffirm, the narrative that you are trying to spin over time. Information from one email could lead to another OPRA request, which could take months to get all of the information to make your case if you are not persistent in following up with the clerk. I recommend that if you have a hunch, make a request that is broad enough not to give your hunch away, but also not too broad that it will be denied as being overly broad.

The hunches that I had when I first began sending OPRA requests for the emails of Delran officials a month prior were about to pay off big time. This time that payoff would come from the emails of the youngest political player in our tale, then 21 year old Colin "The Kid" Rafferty, who was elected to Delran's School Board at just 18, and who the Township administration was about to throw under the bus.

5 Things you need to know about

the Delran Debacle. 11-13-21

The Debacle in Delran prepares to come to a head this Tuesday as the Town Council meets for the first time since the fiery meeting on November 9th when the Council was asked nearly a dozen times if they had received any quotes above the bidding threshold of $44,000 that included both the video and staging services, yet they refused to answer. It was like a scene out A Few Good Men as I barked the question over and over like I was Tom Cruise questioning Jack Nicholson, but instead of old Col. Jessup ordering a code red, it was Solicitor Sal who allegedly ordered NJ's youngest political player, Colin Rafferty, to split the bids to circumvent the RFP process. That Township Council meeting video for 11-09-21 has been viewed nearly 700 times on the town's YouTube page in just 2 weeks, so it's obvious people are interested, but how did it get to this point?

1. This has never been about Carli Lloyd or the need for her to be celebrated by the town. So what is this all about?

The Debacle in Delran has always been about the financial records, documents and information that the Township has failed to accurately provide and or have been purposely omitted to cover up what is now a clear case of corruption. When I first got involved in this it was merely to answer one simple question, "How Much Did Delran Spend On The Carli Lloyd Celebration?". Once that article was posted on the Town's most popular FaceBook page, Delran Residents Official, some people took it the wrong way, and all hell broke loose. People were attacking me from all sides. One of those people was the Town's own Mayor, Gary Catrambone, who on 10-19-21, created a post that made claims about a non-resident (Me) that was making claims of bribery and coercion as it pertained to a donor to the event, who also happened to have an outstanding variance application that was set to be heard just a week later, but the variance hearing was postponed until a later date after the false allegations set forth by the Mayor created what some could see as an appearance of impropriety, which is something I had never alleged.

2. How much did the Carli Lloyd celebration actually cost?

When I asked for all costs for the event I was given a printout that shows $37,633.88 in costs, a number that should have included all of the costs, but for some reason, it didn't. After some folks complained that the numbers I released didn't include any of the donations that were given by the Township, I again asked the clerk to send me all costs plus all donations received. The clerk sent me back a spreadsheet showing that the costs had now changed to a lower number and there were certain services listed that were not listed on the original spreadsheet, in particular, a company called Go Events. The costs on the new spreadsheet equaled roughly $28,000 in costs and the donations received were roughly $35,000, but as we learned at the 10-26-21 Delran Council work session, the costs were actually $90,456 to throw the event and the donations were $46,166. However, the $90,456 in costs still does not include the hundreds of overtime hours for the Police Department nor for the Public Works Department. So the costs of the 2.5 hour event were well over $100,000 for an event that brought out maybe 200 guests!

3. Is Go Events connected to Delran Mayor Gary Catrambone? If so, how?

Go Events is the company that the Township paid $5950 to hire a band and DJ for the retirement celebration. When I noticed that the Township had omitted Go Events from their first response, and when I realized that the Delran Mayor runs his own DJ company, I felt that looking into Go Events could lead to a conflict of interest, which it did. It turns out it is the Mayor's own Nephew Frank Catrambone, who owns Go Events. Frank is not only the Mayor's nephew, but he is also the Mayor's boss at Center Stage Entertainment, a company that is registered at the same address as Go Events. Interestingly, even though he was listed as "Center Stage's original DJ", Mayor Gary Catrambone's page was deleted from the Center Stage Entertainment website after the Mayor admitted that Go Events was owned by his nephew at the 11-9-21 meeting.

Alex Glover also works for Center Stage Entertainment, and he was one of the people seeking quotes on behalf of the township for the retirement party. Alex was accepting quotes on behalf of the Township as a representative of Center Stage Entertainment, the company Mayor Gary Catrambone lists first on his financial disclosure statement as one of his employers. Not only was Alex Glover seeking quotes on behalf of the township as a representative of the same company that the Mayor works for and his nephew owns, Alex is also the person who signed the contract on behalf of Go Events with the Township's Administrator, Jeff Hatcher. This makes him not just the seeker of services that he is negotiating on behalf of the township for, but he is also the vendor of the services. That's also how he negotiated such a great deal on behalf of the taxpayers by using their money to pay $5950 for the DJ and a cover band.

4. Did the Township have any contracts that included both the staging and video services that were above the bidding threshold of $44,000? If so, were those contracts split?

Many might wonder why I asked the Township Council and Solicitor if they received any contracts that included both the video and staging services that were above $44,000, and more importantly, why they wouldn't answer? It's simple, bid splitting is not only unethical, it is illegal. Bid splitting is a form of procurement fraud against the government, and hence, against the taxpayers. Bidding thresholds are safeguards put in place so large scale projects have more scrutiny and have less of an opportunity for corruption. Title 40A – MUNICIPALITIES AND COUNTIES Section 40A:11-7 – Contracts not to be divided, states that "no contract...shall be divided, so as to bring it or any of the parts thereof under the bid threshold", but that is exactly what was done in this situation, not just once, but twice.

The truth is that the Township and or its entertainment consultant didn't just have one quote that included both the video and staging services above the bidding threshold, they actually had 4 of them. Two were from Starlite, with one being for $150,000 and another being for $61,500, both including video and staging services in each contract. The other Two were from Spellcaster, with one for $61,804 and the other being $59,593, both again including the video and staging services in each contract.

As you may have read in the emails acquired from the Township, Colin Rafferty wrote to a representative from Starlite that they were "having an issue with the bidding threshold", which at that point they were working with a contract that was cut down from $150,000 to $61,500, which was still well over the bidding threshold of 44K. Colin then goes on in the next email to say that the Solicitor directed him that "It must be two separate contracts", referring to the staging and video services that were then broken into two separate service contracts, one being for $39,000 from Starlite, and the other being for $22,500 from Video Walltronics, even though both services were already offered in one by Starlite for the exact same amount of $61,500.

The second example of bid splitting comes from the company that placed the lowest of the quotes for both services but for some reason was rejected, Spellcaster, who was more than capable of handling the event. Spellcaster has thrown thousands of concerts and events, including some of the biggest names in show business, so they had the right credentials. Spellcaster, just like Starlite, actually put in three quotes. Two included both the staging and video services, which were both above the bidding threshold, and one that only included the staging services, which was for $34,165.

The other quote that Alex Glover received on behalf of the Township for the video services was from a company called Kathedral Event Center, which was for $25,215, yet when I looked through Kathedral's website I couldn't find anything about them renting giant video screens. That is because the Kathedral Event Center is just that, it's an event center that holds weddings and other large scale events, but it doesn't rent video screens trailers. So why would Kathedral Event Center write a quote for the same video screens that were already being offered by Spellcaster? Well I'd bet that's probably due to the fact that both companies are owned by the same person.

5. What's next? Tuesday night's political showdown in Delran!

If you have been paying attention to the events throughout the Delran Debacle, you would know that the last two public council meetings have been turning points in my investigations. At the 10-26 meeting we finally learned that the actual costs of the event were not the $37,633 that the township first reported, but they were at least $90,456, which still didn't include Police and Public Works. At the 11-9 meeting we finally learned just how Frank Catrambone is related to the mayor, which was that he was both his boss and his nephew. So what will we learn at the 11-23 meeting?

Will Council President Burrell or the Solicitor answer as to why the Township received at least 4 contracts above the 44K threshold that included all services that were later split? Will the Solicitor respond to the questions raised by the emails from Colin Rafferty that claimed the Solicitor directed him to split the contract from Starlite into two contacts after Colin openly admitted to having an "issue with the bidding threshold"?

Will the Mayor explain why the township hired his nephew's company for the inflated cost of $5950 for a DJ and a Band, or why his co-worker is negotiating on behalf of the town? Will Jeff Hatcher tell us why he was the one who ordered Go Events and allowed the Mayor's co-worker Alex Glover at Center Stage Entertainment, to both negotiate on behalf of the town at the same time that he was signing as the representative for Go Events?

These questions and more will surely be asked at this Tuesday's anticipated council meeting, whether they will be answered will be a whole other story.

Transcript From November 23rd, 2021 Delran Council Meeting.

Duff: Hello my name is Patrick Duff. Formerly 812 Chester avenue. I'm a Haddon Heights resident. Like I said before, I'd rather not state the actual address. I'm kind of like a nomadic warrior, I consider myself. I like to go to different towns.

Last time we were here, obviously there was a little bit of excitement, a little commotion. Some questions were asked and they weren't answered. I asked the question if there were contracts that were above $44 000 that included both services? Everybody refused to answer that question. Some people said they were concept proposals. But there were four. There were four contracts that included all services. One was $150,000, one was $61,500, another one was $61,804, and another for $59,000 and some change. All of them included all services.

Now I do a lot of OPRA requests, and I did an OPRA for the emails from the Township. And I said hey, I'd like to take a look and see what's happening here, you know? And the only emails I received back were from Colin Rafferty. Not from Tyler, not from the Mayor, not from any of the Council people, I requested everybody's emails. But Collin's came back, and Colin's email is pretty clear that on I believe it was September 25th. or 26th, he said that they were "having an issue with the bidding threshold." At that point the quote that they had, that they were working on, that literally the person is saying "hey if you don't accept this quote now, if you don't get this going, I can't save these employees for you for that date." So it wasn't a concept! It was a person trying to gain business for their company, and a person negotiating on behalf of the Township. That person then says "we're having an issue with the bidding threshold".

First question is, what would that issue have been since the bidding threshold is $44,000, and the bid was at $61,500, we could figure that the issue might be the fact that the issue is the bidding threshold is almost twenty thousand dollars less? Because in the next email he goes on to say that "the solicitor told him to separate the quotes". Now the other word for separate, would be split. So literally, split the quotes up. Split the contracts.

They took the exact same services, nothing different, the video services and the staging services, which cost $61,500 when they were grouped together. Were separated, or split, for the exact cost again. $22,500 for the video, and $39,000 for the staging and audio services. Now if you look at procurement fraud red flags, or red flags for bid rigging, one of the main red flags is these even numbers. $150,000, $39,000, $61,500, you know, there's no dollars and cents there, just a straight number. So that's one of the red flags. Another red flag is contracts that somebody gets, that then get split into multiple contracts, as has happened here. The second company, Spellcaster, that didn't get the bids, had a $61,000 bid, a $59,000 bid, then they gave you a $34,000 bid just for the stage in the audio.

The bid was from Kathedral Event Center, which by the way Kathedral, they do events like weddings. You know, a big event venue, but they don't rent video trailers. So that's why the quote that's from Kathedral is interesting, because you'd say "well, why would Kathedral rent video trailers when that's not what they do?".

Well that's because the owner of Spellcaster is the owner of Kathedral. So he just took another letterhead and wrote his quote on that to try and satisfy the Township, but you were getting the same exact services. So to say you didn't split the services doesn't make any sense. You did. To say that you didn't have any quotes above $44,000 is a lie that included all services.

And to release only Collins emails, I think is cowardly. I do. I think it's cowardly. You release a 21 year old kid's emails, who was clear in these emails that he incriminated himself. and you didn't release your own emails. I think that's cowardly.

So, two questions, number one. Did you receive any quotes or proposals above $44,000 that included both services? That question was just answered. And number two, what did Colin mean when he said he was having an "issue with the bidding threshold", what was that issue? And Sal, did you tell him to separate the services?

Sal Siciliano: (upset) Well sir, my name is Mr. Sicilano.

Duff: OK, Mr Siciliano. By the way, no offense, go back in the videos. He calls you Solicitor Sal. He calls the Solicitor, Sal. Everybody here calls you Solicitor Sal. Your name's not very easily said, "Solicitor Siciliano". Try saying that three times fast, you couldn't do it. But I'm asking you a serious question. Did you have the young man separate the quotes?

Sal: Sir, my name is Solicitor Siciliano.

Duff: Did you have them separate the quotes?

Sal: I'm not going to answer that question. There's no reason to answer that question. So I'm not going to answer.

Duff: I'm being very reasonable, I'm calm.

Burrell: Mr. Duff do you mind if I..

Sal: You've answered your own question.

Duff: So you did have them split the quotes?

Sal: I never said that.

Burrell: Mr Duff, can you address me real quick please.

Duff: Yes sir.

Burrell: You can have a conversation, that's why you're here. Let's, let's have a dialogue, and a public comment, that's appropriate, So, one, I just have to clear up. All my emails were given to the clerks and under review by the Solicitor's office. That is the process that's being taken care of right now. I did it immediately, all of my emails are being reviewed, and will be provided. There was no grand conspiracy to release Collin's earlier than anybody else's. I'm not sure how that happened, but I can promise you. I'm not involved in how OPRA requests get sent out. I give them to the clerk and the Solicitor's office and they take care of it. All my records have been produced. So I just want to clear that up for the record. But, Sal do you mind explaining the, there's a lot of terms that are being used that aren't actually what they, you know, each term has a specific meaning. Can you just explain the procurement process broadly about what's going on so we can set the record straight?

Sal: I'm, I'm, I'm happy to. The procurement process is very broad. The Township has an opportunity to retain services in a number of different manners. Negotiations, quotes, all of those go to the procurement process. What is ultimately selected, what is ultimately contracted, that's uh, uh, the final issue with regard to contracting and local public contract law. As I've stated before. No, no laws were broken. All the laws were followed. We followed every process. We followed every procedure, we've continued to do so. We are doing so with regard to the OPRA requests, which are being reviewed right now.

The methodology for the review of the OPRA request is, as they were produced, or as the requests were received, as they were produced to the clerk. They were then sent to my office. It is a first in, first out, chronological process. I can assure you there's been a substantial amount of time devoted to the review of those emails. Uh, your emails are being reviewed at this time, Council President. All the members of Council, whoever produced those, are going through those methodically, chronologically, as is the need to do so.

Um, no I'm not going to answer a question with regard to the meaning or the intent of an email, or what's written down. That's not the purpose of an OPRA request. We're not mind readers, we don't read minds, we don't, we don't do that at all. But I can categorically state that there has been no, um, illegal actions taken with regard to the public contracting. I'm very confident in making that statement.

Burrell: All right thank you Sal. And um, the other, the other question was that, is it safe to say that your office was involved in the procurement process?

Sal: Yes.

Burrell: And your office reviewed everything, and was aware of the entire process?

Sal: Yeah

Duff: Could I just please ask a simple question? Because Solicitor Siciliano, you had mentioned last week that you did not know if there was a company that could offer both services when a citizen asked you that question. If you're involved in the process, you would have known that. Isn't that correct?

Sal: I don't believe I made that statement. I disagree with that question.

Barb Littleton from the audience: It was my question, and you did!

Duff: You did.

Sal: I don't recall that.

Barb Littleton: Go back and listen.

Duff: I've listened to it about four times. You definitely made that statement. So the question I have is, were there contracts that included both services above $44,000 that were prior to the contracts that were separated?

Sal: Again, I don't recall, I don;t recall, I don't recall that.

Duff: No. I'm asking you a question now.

Sal: Sir, and I am trying to, I don't know, again, I don't recall that. That's my answer.

Duff: No, It's a simple question. Were there four bids above $44,000 that included both services, Solicitor?

Sal: Sir, I am not going to answer your question. I don't recall the answer.

Duff: I feel like this is Bill Clinton here.

Sal: You can characterize me however you want. (audience murmuring)

Duff: Seriously. Come on. And my last and final comment is, Mr. Catrambone and Tyler, you both had some very telling, um you know, remarks about campaigning. You said, Mr.Catrambone, that you're eager to build your dedication to transparency in new ways as the mayor. In addition to live streaming the meetings, he plans to hold small group sessions so residents may understand how decisions get made, and take a more active role in their local government. People have been asking questions for weeks. You refuse to answer.

Transparent? You're translucent. You can't see what's going on in this Council, it's sad. Mr. Burrell you went on to say that you actually built the website for Delran, and that you feel proud that the transparency of the governing body, by creating this live streaming service is something good for the citizens. But you still refuse to answer these questions. I mean, I'm asking a direct question. And nobody's, and no offense (pointing to the other Council members) this side of the room it doesn't even seem like you have a mouth! You haven't said a word in the three weeks I've been here.

So, were there, maybe you could answer this? Were there quotes above $44,000 that included all services? Then I'm done, I'm done by the way. You guys will not see me again for a while. I'll get the emails and stuff, but I'm gonna go move on to something different and this will be ,uh, the last time you see me for a while. So I'm sure you'll probably have some drinks on that.

Delran's Solid Waste Contract Increased by 45%! 12-7-21

Delran Mayor Gary Catrambone's 9-29-21 message to the Township brought the bad news of a significant increase in the solid waste contract that was signed the previous evening by Council President Tyler Burrell and Delran's Clerk, Jamey Eggers. The contract was awarded to the only bidder, Republic Services, for $822,030 for just the first year, which is a 45% increase from the previous amount of $458,892 for the prior year of trash collection services. In the Township's statement they claim that "The Township sent bid packages out to all the major trash companies that service this area and allowed a 60-day response period to promote competition." But that does not seem to be the case from the emails provided by the Township through an OPRA request.

The emails provided by the Township show a much different story, with a total of 9 emails sent or received on behalf of the Solid Waste bidding process, most of them being companies asking for the bid specifications, which should have been available online, but were not. Four of the emails requested bid packages, four others were returning the bid packages to the companies, and one was a company saying thank you to the Township. While the Township did respond with bid packages, they did not do so until July 8th, some 9 days after the request for proposals were issued by the Township, leaving only 51 days to submit a bid.

On August 5th a mysterious email was sent to the Township from a reporter from NJ.com, Linda O'Brien, asking if Delran is planning a homecoming celebration for the world renowned soccer star, Carli Lloyd. I say it is mysterious due to the fact that it wasn't until 9 days later that Carli Lloyd announced her retirement to the world, yet from this email one can assume that the planning for the retirement party had already begun.

Hundreds of emails were sent and received over the next two months regarding the planning of the retirement party, all done while the solid waste bids were all but forgotten about.

Ironically, on the very same day that the Solid Waste Bids were due of August 31st, the Township received its first proposal from Starlite, the company that Delran hired to provide the stage, audio and lighting for the retirement party. The $150,000 proposal was for a stage, lighting, audio and video services for a two and a half hour party in a small town. That proposal would later be decreased to $61,500, but in a chain of emails between Starlite and Colin Rafferty, that amount still created an "issue with the bidding threshold" and Colin asked for a call "immediately." In an email just 4 days later Colin wrote that the Township's Solicitor, Sal Siciliano, "has directed me that it must be two separate contracts. Will that be a problem?".

The contracts were then split in two so the "issue with the bidding threshold" that Colin had mentioned, was not an issue anymore.

What was an issue at that same time was the fact that Delran had only received one bid for the solid waste contract, a contract that the Township claimed "The time has come to award the contract, as this is a necessary service that MUST be provided to our residents, and it is regrettable that only one company submitted a bid."But was that really the case?

In January of 2020 Moorestown NJ was faced with a similar situation when the company that provides their solid waste service exercised their right not to extend the option in their contract with the town, yet at that point the township did not have enough time for the 60 days required to put out a proposal for a public bid. Moorestown requested a 30 day extension from Central Jersey Waste so they could have enough time to legally seek competitive bids to get the best deal on behalf of their tax payers, and Central Jersey Waste agreed. After the 60 day period two bids were submitted to Moorestown, one from Central Jersey Waste and one from Republic Services, with the Township choosing Central Jersey waste for an increase of about 20% over the previous contract year.

Moorestown has a population of 20,355, and Delran has a population of 16,524, which is roughly 81% of Moorestown's population. Delran's 3 year contract with Republic Service totals $2,566,052, which is 9% higher than the 3 year total for Moorestown's solid waste contract even though Delran has 19% less population. One would think that less people equals less cost, but in this case it is clear that it does not. While Delran claimed they were reaching out to all of the trash companies in the area seeking bids, they were actually seeking donations to plan a party that, once you read the schedule, can only be seen as a Democratic campaign event.

A total of 12 politicians graced the $39,000 stage for the two and a half hour party that wound up costing well over $100,000, held conveniently just 2 weeks before the election. As dozens of invitations were being sent to politicians, and numerous donations were being sought from local businesses and even major organizations such as Nike regarding a two hour party, the solid waste contract that was looming was not even a thought. Instead of the Township worrying about a multi-million dollar 3 year contract that should have been their priority, they were worried about giving inflated contracts to the mayor's nephew and figuring out how to split the contracts so they can circumvent the law to throw their shindig before the election.

Transcript From December 7th, 2021 Delran Council Meeting.

Duff: (In a fresh ass suit) Good evening, how are you guys doing? Patrick Duff, Haddon Heights.

It's been the 4th week I've been back in Delran, and I love the town of Delran. I tell you, that's why I'm doing this. I wouldn't have spent as much time in any other town if I was investigating. I usually do big cities, things like that are going to be in the national news. Now the town of Delran was on the news today. You were in WHYY, and not one of you made a comment in your comment section. That's sad. I mean, come on you were literally put on news, with allegations of bid splitting, allegations of nepotism, and conflicts of interest. Yet in your comments you refused to even acknowledge it.

You ran on an air of transparency. Imagine that? You said you're going to be the most transparent Council in Delran's history. If that's true, then what were the other councils?

Was the door even open? Could people even watch? So I have a couple questions actually um.. (going back to grab an agenda to use as a prop)

So on August 30th, you were CC to an email that had a contract from Starlight for $150,000. So I'm just going to use these as an example. So you had one contract, or quote...

Burrell: Mr Duff before you begin, it was not a contract.

Duff: Okay, what would you call it?

Burrell: It was a proposal.

Duff: Okay, What do you do a request for proposals for? You do request for proposals so you can get a proposal, so then you can either accept it or not, correct?

Burrell: Yes.

Duff: So it was a proposal, correct?

Burrell: So it was a proposal, correct. It was not in response to a request for proposal, but..

Duff: What was it in response to?

Burrell: A call to Starlight and asked for what it would cost?

Duff: Okay, so do you agree that there was one contract for $150,000.

Burrell: No. I agree there was a proposal,

Duff: One proposal, you'll call it a proposal right?

Burrell: Sure.

Duff: Would you agree that there was a second , by the way, when I asked for all quotes from the Township, the Township only sent me the quotes that were below the $44,000 threshold? Is that correct, Mr. Burrell?

Burrell: I don't know. I wasn't privy to that OPRA request. I believe you.

Duff: When I, at the two meetings ago, I then produced that contract that I received from a third party, and then I was sent the other contracts. Which were supposed to be all the contracts that were above the $44,000 threshold, right? But just today, I swear to god today I received another OPRA response that shows that there was not just one, there was not just two, but there were three contracts from Starlight that were above $44,000, or proposals, the second one being for $73,500. Were you aware of that, Mr. Burrell?

Burrell: Uh, no.

Duff: Were you aware of that, Mr. Hatcher?

Town Manager Jeff Hatcher: No

Duff: Okay, we have two proposals, $150,000, and $73,500. (placing two pieces of paper on the table as examples) The third proposal was for $61,500 from Starlight. Tyler you were cc'd to this, you were CC'd to this, Mayor you, and were CC'd to this Mr. Hatcher.

Hatcher: I don't believe I was.

Duff: I apologize if you weren't. Were you aware that there was a third contract, or a third proposal from Starlight for $61,500. So you (Hatcher) never saw the proposal for $61,500?

Hatcher: No.

Duff: Okay so the fourth contract that came from Starlight was for $39,000, were you aware of this contract?

Hatcher: Yes.

Duff: Did you also help Delran acquire staging services in 2019?

Did you sign a purchase order for stage services from SLM entertainment for $9,602?

Hatcher: I can't recall.

Duff: Okay, I can say you did. The stage was $9,602. As a qualified purchasing agent, isn't it your job to make sure that the items that are being bought, are the value in which they are supposed to be?

Hatcher: I have no involvement.

Burrell: Jeff can you just turn your mic on for the record?

Hatcher: I have no involvement in dealing directly with these vendors. I don't have any knowledge of stages, or video. There were other people that were doing that, not me.

Duff: I thought you were involved in everything in a town? It was just said that you know every little in and out in this town.

Hatcher: Sir I,I, don't, I... my department heads go out and they purchase equipment and they come back to me. They get the quotes, items along those lines, I look at them, if they meet it, I'm fine with it. They'll explain to me what's going on. That's what happened in this instance, there were people they were put in charge of acquiring those items. I know nothing about stages, or lighting, or any of those items at all.

Duff: Can you please explain to the Township of Delran. Do you know what bid splitting is?

Hatcher: I know what bid splitting is, but...

Duff: Is it illegal?

Hatcher: I believe it's illegal, but I also don't think, again, I wasn't asked the question and nor were these bids, and that's what you need to understand. I know we don't want to bring that issue in, and I wasn't asked a question. So I don't know what conversation took place between Colin and the Solicitor, but these were not bids. and bid splitting is usually when you take volumes of an item, and you split it to get below. These are not volumes of items. I don't know if it were brought to me, I would have sent it to the Solicitor, because I wouldn't have known the answer either, because these were separate items. It was video boards, lighting, and stages. That's not cutting in half volumes of an item.

Duff: Would you agree that if there was a contract that included all these items, would you agree that there was the contract above $44,000 that included all these items, that was then, remember, a $61,500 contract (tearing a piece of paper) was torn in two. one half for video services, one for the audio on stage. Would you agree that, if that happened, that would be considered bid splitting?

Hatcher: I honestly don't know.

Duff: So just to be clear here. The fact is that while all this is going on you're planning the party for Carli Lloyd, and hundreds of emails are being sent on behalf of the Township, literally. Letters to every business in Delran seeking donations. Yet the only produced emails for the entire trash contract that the Township can produce, are nine. Now I find that, and as you said, "it's a very important contract for the Township." You say that you had to go with the one bid and on the Township it says that you must basically go with the service. Could the Township have extended the contract for a 60-day period and sought new bids from other companies?

Burrell: The answer to that is yes. But if we had one bidder for the first...(being stopped and interrupted by Jeff Hatcher)

Hatcher: I don't, excuse me. I don't think it was going to be a "yes". (Commotion amongst the Council members)

Burrell: um well you'd have to get it...

Duff: So there's a disagreement here?

Hatcher: The contractor, the contractor, was losing hundreds of thousands of dollars each year on Delran. I had a conversation after the bid came in, and I spoke with the contractor and said "can you explain this to me because I've never seen anything like this" and he said he was losing hundreds of thousands of dollars each of the last three years on Delran. That COVID was a major issue in terms of addressing this issue, is that they couldn't get their equipment, they couldn't get personnel, anybody who manages a business knows what businesses went through trying to get personnel and equipment. And they were losing money on Delran, and um that we have a liberal bulk pickup that you can't compare it to a town that gets it once a month. We have it every week. People can put bulk pickup out and we have a higher level of service so you need to look at those things. But I agree the contract came in high. But we bid it legally. We didn't have any other option at that point in time because there's a 60-day, not a 30-day, there's a 60-day requirement to advertise.

Duff: That being said, with the sixty-day requirement, could you have asked for an extension on the current contract that you had to extend it?

Hatcher: They weren't going to extend it. I spoke with them, they were not going to extend it. They were losing money.

Duff: So Moorestown, though, extended the contract. They were able to do that.

Burrell: They got permission from their vendor.

Duff: yeah and is there, is there..

Hatcher: Okay, a completely different situation, We had a contract coming to an end. They had a contract that had three years with a two-year extension. Their contractor came to them and said, we don't want to go for the next two years. It put them

72

in a hole where they didn't have time to advertise it, and they said they were willing to extend it at a higher rate for 30 days because Moorestown was letting them out of the contract. It's a completely different situation than what we had.

Duff: The last question is, the Township said that they sent bid proposals to all the trash companies in the area and allowed for a 60-day period for them to respond. But in the emails it's clear that the companies reached out to the Township. and maybe the clerk can verify this and said that the bid proposals were not available online, like they legally should have been, and that the bid proposals were not sent to the vendors until July 8th. That's when the clerk sent the bid proposals. So the Township in fact, did not reach out to any trash companies themselves. The trash companies reached out to the Township seeking proposals, I'm sorry seeking bid specifications that should have been available online. So did the Township in fact reach out to all these companies, and if they did, where are the emails, and is there an email to prove or a correspondence to prove that you had this conversation with Republic regarding the trash contract?

Hatcher: I have an email with a memo, I don't know that, I provided...

Burrell: Mr. Duff there's an email with a memo there that's been provided.

Duff: I've had nothing provided.

Burrell: As I mentioned to your friend over there about the conversations. That they were provided and the three vendors that we sent the bid specs to, and two of them chose not to that's, that's the answer.

Duff: They reached out to us though, isn't that correct? For the bids?

Burrell: We did not reach out to them, correct. That's correct, thank you.

Duff: Do you think that the Township did a service to the community by sending only nine emails on behalf of the trash contract, but hundreds on behalf of Carli Lloyd?

Burrell: All right, I don't agree with that assessment, your assessment.

Duff: Do you think that that is a good use of the Township's time?

Burrell: Mr Duff, the trash contract is...entering into contracts to that extent is something that's an ordinary course for the business for the Township. Putting on the Carli Lloyd retirement party is not something that happens every day, and there's not a playbook that we pull off the shelf and go through. If you're gonna let me, you ask questions, you're gonna get responses. Do you understand? So can you please let me answer your questions. So, you know there is going to be more emails, there's more people involved, more departments involved in putting together an event, in you know a month and a half time than an ordinary course of a contract. That probably Jeff and the administration have awarded hundreds of contracts you know, not hundreds of trash contracts, but a handful of trash contracts, and significant contracts in the past. So the amount of emails that are sent, I understand, I understand your question, but I don't think the amount of emails that are sent determine the gravity of, of, a situation or the importance of it.

Duff: I think what it determines is the effort that the Council made, and the Mayor made, and the administration made on behalf of the people of Delran to achieve the best result in a three-year contract. When you want to achieve the best result in a two and a half hour party, which includes giving contracts to nephews, including uh taking two contracts which you will not admit, which is...Can I ask you just a real quick question? The $61,500 proposal, what was different between the $61,500

74

proposal and the $39,000 proposal?

Burrell: I don't know off the top of my head.

Duff: You should be able to answer that. One was a "concept proposal". What was the next one that you signed a contract for?

Burrell: I don't know the difference between the two, and we didn't sign a contract for $61,500.

Duff: You signed it for $39,000 and then you signed one for $22,500. The same exact amount. Isn't that true?

Burrell: Yeah.

Duff: For the same services as the $61,500 contract, isn't that true?

Burrell: No, no, they're different services, Mr. Duff.

Duff: I mean it's listed on the contract, Mr. Burrell. You know what's sad, this is so sad, that you've been presented with this evidence that's in front of your face' and you refuse to listen. This is the problem with America, is that people are so partisan that if somebody smacked him in the face with a turd, and it was their own Party member. They would just look the other way. But you're all being smacked in the face with a turd right now and none of you are saying anything. I say shame on you, Shame on all of you for not making a comment about being put in the paper. Shame on all of you for not admitting when you're wrong, because you were wrong, and if you can't answer the questions then it's obvious that you're guilty.

Burrell: Thank you Mr Duff.

CHAPTER 6
The Shakedown

As you just saw, even when asked the same question, Mr. Burrell and Mr. Hatcher had two totally different answers as to whether the original trash contract could have been extended. Burrell said yes, which was the truth. Yet, Hatcher immediately claimed otherwise in an attempt to cover his own ass, because as the Township's administrator he was the one responsible for both advertising and receiving the bids.

Both Burrell and Hatcher also claimed they were not aware of any of the quotes above $44,000, and only were aware of the contacts below the $44,000 threshold needed to seek a public bid. But that's impossible considering I had just been sent the three contracts that were above $44,000 from the Township. So how could the Council President and Township Manager not know about the contracts that I was sent from the Township?

What's even more odd is that both Colin and Tyler were recruited as young kids to work with Gary as party DJ's, who at the time was in his mid 40's. Then they both got elected as the youngest people in the history of NJ to their respective positions, all with DJ Gary Cat by their side. So how could Tyler say he didn't know Gary worked at Center Stage? Gary had worked for Center Stage Entertainment since the company's inception, yet now he was also claiming he didn't work for them? His bio page at Center Stage Entertainment had been in existence for decades, but the day after I printed the story showing Gary gave a contract to his family member, it suddenly disappeared.

An article written by April Saul from WHYY was printed on the morning of the December 7th Council meeting regarding the Delran Debacle. The article broke down my findings for the spending on the Carli Lloyd party, as well as things such as the Mayor not informing the Council about him hiring an events company that was owned by his nephew, which caused quite the stir in the small town.

While Delran's administration had been keeping a strong public front, the revelation that Gary Cat's nephew owned Go Events was enough for the local political party to ask Gary to either give back the $5,950, or resign. Gary agreed to give the $5,950 back instead of resigning during a meeting held at Lying Lynn Jeney's basement. But minutes prior to the next Council session, Gary broke his promise and refused to give the money back, and he also refused to resign.

While I did not know about Gary agreeing to give the money back and then declining to do so at this point in the battle, I did see a rift begin to appear in Council and Gary Cat, specifically from Council President Burrell. Nobody from Delran's Council would speak to me at the time, so I figured I'd extend a private branch of communication to Burrell, an invitation that he wisely accepted. For Burrell this was one of his best political moves, because his willingness to communicate, even if it were just in private, caused me to be much easier on him over the next couple of months than I should have been.

Not long after posting the trash contract story and showing my proof that Sal told Colin to split the contracts to avoid the bidding threshold, people started to see that I was showing the receipts, while the township was bumbling over themselves trying to respond to my inquiries. This brought out some tips from the community on what to look into next, with one Facebook comment just saying, "I wish Duff would look into what happened to Dunphy.", but it was quickly erased. Which only intrigued me more.

This caused me to jump into action to see if I could find anything in the minutes and or agendas that had anything to do with "Dunphy". After only a couple of minutes of searching I found a resolution approving a settlement between Delran Township and Dunphy's Landscaping. The resolution listed 23 separate torts, including RICO violations, extortion, abuse of power and unlawful taking. The resolution was approving a settlement to avoid a lawsuit, only there was no monetary amount listed as to what the township paid to Dunpy, which is generally required for such a resolution.

I figured that I could find something if I watched the video of the Council meeting where the resolution was approved, and boy was I right. Council President Tyler Burrell read a statement into the record where he revealed that the Township was paying Dunphy $300,000 to settle the claims. While Delran officials had a policy to post all statements that were read into the record on their website and FaceBook pages, the one about the $300,000 settlement is the only one that just happened to never be posted.

The many cover-ups Delran officials were performing were not just about a pricey political party or shitty trash contracts anymore, this was now about covering up some extremely serious criminal allegations, as well as the payment to make the allegations go away. Once I realized that a settlement had been reached I searched NJ Superior Court's website and I found the absolutely shocking statement of the owner of Dunphy's Landscaping, Jim Dunphy.

Statement of Jim Dunphy
12-14-21

I have spent the last 12 months trying to figure out why my Zoning Permit was revoked and why I have been the target of Delran Township officials, while other landscaping companies located right across the street are able to operate their business in the same A-1 Zone, without a zoning permit, without a mercantile license, and without a use variance. On one occasion last January when Zoning Officer Reimel made his first unannounced inspection, I personally asked him why he revoked the permit and what was going on. He responded that he issued the permit in good faith believing it to be "merited" but was subsequently pressured by Delran Township officials to revoke the permit. I asked him to explain, and he refused, indicating "I need 5 more years of employment to reach retirement" and "do not want to get in the middle of this.".

Following that disturbing conversation, I have been trying to figure out what Mr. Reimel meant by "the middle of this" because my livelihood depends on it. I submit this Certification to advise the Court what I have recently learned the answer to this question. I respectfully request this Court to consider this new information in assessing whether the Delran Zoning Board denied my use variance application in an arbitrary, capricious and unreasonable manner.

By way of a specific recent example, the Zoning Board attorney wrote to this Court on December 9 and 10 about snow removal equipment he thought suddenly appeared. A true copy of these letters are attached hereto as **Exhibit "A."** It's disturbing that photos were taken and letters written the same day I moved the plows out of storage so that I could transport them to my Edgewater Park rental property. What is more disturbing is that the mayor-elect of Delran, Gary Catrambone, who wanted to purchase my property for Delran open space and to open a Delran Historical Society site, came to my property in the middle of the work day on December 9, to take the photographs that were submitted to this Court by letter dated December 10. Therefore, while I am submitting this Certification to respond to the "disturbing facts" raised because they are untrue, I am also submitting this Certification because the Court should be aware of the truly disturbing facts I observed when the mayor elect appeared at my property on December 9 at 3:50 PM.

Mr. Catrambone showed up at my property on December 9, 2020 at approximately 3:50 PM, dressed in black and acting coyly in order to take pictures of my property without being noticed. When we noticed this happening, we asked him who he was and what he was doing. The male, fitting the description of Gary Catrambone, indicated that he was "Gary." When we asked if he was Gary Catrambone, he said yes, that we had a "beautiful" property and that he was there taking photos at the request of the Zoning Board attorney. Mr. Catrambone quickly walked away from us, crossed the street, and was observed making several phone calls. He then was picked up by a person driving a light blue Mercedes who we recognized as Paul Buzzi, Jr., our neighbor located at 4205 Bridgeboro Road and Vice President of the Delran Historical Society. This past June, Mr. Buzzi delivered a written letter to Delran residents urging them to appear and object to my Use Variance Application on June 30 because of our "illegal operations.".

This incident on December 9, where the mayor-elect of Delran personally showed up on my property, on Township time, to take pictures of snow plows that I had just moved out from storage in order to move them to my rental property raises the question whether Mr. Catrambone exerted influence on the Zoning Board in connection with my Use Variance Application, or on Delran zoning officials regarding my permit, cease and desist orders, municipal citations or public opposition to my Use Variance Application with Paul Buzzi, Jr or other residents. In order to assess whether the denial of my Use Variance Application was arbitrary, capricious or unreasonable, I call to the Court's attention the many other landscaping companies like mine, located next door and within blocks of mine, that are allowed to operate their business without a mercantile license, a zoning permit or a use variance in the A-1 Zone while I am harassed by the Township. Why is Pica Landscaping, located 20 feet across Bridgeboro Road from my property, permitted to conduct its landscape business in an A-1 Zone and maintain snow equipment in plain sight on its property while Delran officials are clandestinely appearing at my property to take photos and object to my snow equipment? For the record, I am not, and do not plan to use my snow equipment on my property. I was merely getting out the equipment and salt to prepare to move them to my leased property in Edgewater Park. The Delran Township engineer inspected the snow equipment last March.

Adding to the above unanswered questions, I have also just learned about the political relationship between the Delran Zoning Board Chairman, Lynn Jeney, and his Democratic Committee running mate, Gary Catrambone. I learned after Election Day, November 3, 2020, that Mr. Jeney, who ruled on my Use Variance Application on June 30, 2020, was the running mate of Gary Catrambone on the Delran Democratic ticket for Township Council. Mr. Catrambone campaigned on his experience in preserving open space.

Why does Delran allow eight other landscaping companies to conduct business in the A-1 zone where I am located but not me? Is it because my 16 acre property would satisfy the Delran Democratic Committee's goal of preserving open space? This all suggests that I did not get a fair shake before the Delran Zoning Board and that its denial of my Use Variance was arbitrary, capricious or unreasonable.

On Friday, December 4, 2020, I reached out to Kitty Newman, the prior owner of 4101 Bridgeboro Road to ask her why the Township of Delran seemed to have a vendetta toward me and my landscaping company. Ms. Newman disclosed to me for the first time in this conversation that, at the time I expressed an interest in purchasing the Property last year, she had been in discussions with Gary Catrambone, then the Delran Township Council President, about Delran's interest in purchasing the

Property. She told me of Delran's interest in purchasing that property for open space; to use as a site for the Delran Historical Society; additional township parking; and for other reasons. Ms. Newman indicated that Mr. Catrambone was the only representative from Delran handling these discussions and negotiations, which were substantial, through the summer of 2019. Ms. Newman further stated to me that she disclosed to Mr. Catrambone that she was interested in selling the Property to me for my landscaping business, particularly since I was willing to complete the transaction by November 1, 2019, as my landlord was selling the property I was renting at the time and I needed to find a home for my landscaping company. When Ms. Newman disclosed this to Mr. Catrambone, he indicated that Dunphy's Landscaping "would never be able to obtain a permit for the property" and "would never get a variance." I asked Ms. Newman if she would be willing to sign a certification confirming what she had just told me. She indicated that she was uncomfortable getting involved because she did not "want to end up with a defamation of character lawsuit from Catrambone (and I wouldn't put it past him).".

Transcript/Minutes From December 14th, 2021 Delran Council Meeting.

Duff: Good evening, Patrick Duff of Haddon Heights. Formerly 812 Chester avenue.

When I first started coming here was in October, just after there was a Mayor's message put on Delran township's website, and the Mayor's page. That message was to the town about the Carli Llord event, saying there was somebody, a non-resident, claiming there is bribery and coercion regarding a variance.

Could I ask the Council President, I mean this is on the Township page. Who is the non-resident that the Mayor is referring to?

Does the Council know or can the Mayor let us know?

Burrell: I didn't prepare the statement, so.

Duff: Who was the non-resident you referring to, Mayor?

Mayor Catrambone: It was a non-resident that was involved in, I don't like to name people. That's why I said non-resident.

Duff: Was it me, Mayor? Was I the non-resident, Mayor?

Mayor Catrambone: Does that matter to you?

Duff: Yes it does. It matters to my attorney for the defamation suit the township's about to get hit with. You're shaking your head yes? (talking to Tall Tale Tom Lyon) So let's talk about this. So in that statement you said that the Planning Board was unquestionable. That it was some sort of a crime to question the planning board.

I'm going to read the counts, just the counts that were made against the Township. That the Township paid out $300,000 to Dunphy Landscaping, because the ZoningBoard treated him like a second-class citizen. When he was zoned properly to operate a business, and you didn't allow him to operate the business. He was granted a permit, and you took the permit back from him. Okay?

So these are the counts against the Delran Township Zoning Board, which you had said was irrefutable. It's an offense for anybody to say anything bad about them. Civil rights violations, RICO violations, that's racketeering. Delran Township is being accused of racketeering. The Zoning Board, you are being accused of trespass, unlawful taking, interference with quiet enjoyment, harassment, retaliatory conduct, defamation, civil rights violations, retaliation, and abuse of power in office. This is only half of these, this is only half of these. I'm going to read a statement from Jim Dunphy that was in the record for the case against Delran Township for the appeal for the Zoning Board.

Dunphy appealed to the Superior Court and part of his statement, it's disturbing. This is disturbing. I think that if nobody asks you to step down and you don't resign, Mayor, that this Township is in deep trouble.

This is what Jim Dunphy says;

"I have spent the last 12 months trying to figure out why my zoning permit was revoked and why I've been the target of Delran Township officials, while other landscaping companies have been able to operate the same a1 zone without permit, without mercantile license, and without use variants....I am submitting this certification because the court should be aware of a truly disturbing fact that I observed on my property when the mayor-elect gary Catrambone showed up on my property on December 9th, 2020 at approximately 3:50 p.m". Did you do that mayor?

Mayor Catrambone: I did not go on his property.

Duff: Were you taking pictures of Dunphy's property at 3 50 p.m on
December 9th?

Mayor Catrambone: I did not go on his property.

Duff: Were you taking pictures?

Mayor Catrambone: (voice gets high) I did.

Duff: Why?

Mayor Catrambone: Because it was beautiful.

Duff: Why? Why were you taking pictures of his property? Solicitor, did you direct Mayor Catrambone? Because in this statement it says that when the Mayor was asked if he was Gary Catrambone, he said "yes they had a beautiful property that he was taking photos at the request of the Zoning Board attorney". And that's you Mr. Siciliano, right? Did you direct Mr. Catrambone to go get pictures of the Dunphy's property?

(Long pause while Solicitor Sal is refusing to answer)

Duff: Is this real? I'll go on. It says that there was a conversation that Dunphy had with Kitty Newman. Kitty Newman let him know that when Miss Newman said to the Mayor that she was thinking about selling the property to Dunphy, Mayor Catrambone said "he would never be able to obtain a permit for that property and would never get a variance. Did you say that to Miss Kitty Newman Mr. Catrambone?

Mayor Catrambone: I don't remember saying those words. I may have said that it wasn't zoned for that.

Duff: But it is zoned for that, isn't that correct?

Mayor Catrambone: No.

Duff: Are there other landscaping companies operating in the same A1 zone as Dunphy Landscaping?

Mayor Catrambone: That's a different question.

Duff: Are there?

Mayor Catrambone: There are other landscaping companies in the A1 zone, yes.

Duff: Okay, and is Jim Dunphy's property in the A1 zone?

Mayor Catrambone: Yes.

Duff: Did you have an interest in trying to buy that same property for the Delran Historical Society?

Mayor Catrambone: No. We attempted to buy it, the Township attempted to buy it, but it wasn't for the Delran Historical Society.

Duff: What was it for?

Mayor Catrambone: We wanted to preserve the land. The Historical Society had an interest in perhaps making that house a museum. It wasn't for them, or to give to them.

Duff: Now in the resolution that you passed for the Township. Do you realize you did not include the amount of the settlement? The $300,000 was mysteriously left out of your resolution. Now aren't you supposed to include the amount Solicitor, in the resolution of what you paid the....(Burrell interrupting)

Burrell: Mr. Duff, you have one minute remaining, so wrap it up. I want to say this, I respect what you're doing, you're allowed to ask questions in public comment, we appreciate that and there's nothing we're trying to hide. But Mr Duff, this is not a cross-examination.

Duff: Great.

Burrell: You know, please provide what you need to say, and we'll answer your questions at the end. But to answer your direct question. With that, I read into the record a long statement which you have in front of me. I'm sure you've heard me read in the record.

Duff: Correct.

Burrell: And that said the amount that we paid. It was very clear there was no and....

Duff: Does that satisfy the law? The resolution?

Burrell: Ah, Mr. Duff, I'm speaking...

Duff: I'm asking you a question about the written resolution, Tyler.

Burrell: I don't recall what the resolution said at the time. It was drafted between our administration and our Solicitor' office.

Duff: My question is, do resolutions need to include the amount of the settlement agreement when you make one with a party?

Burrell: I don't know that question, that'd be a question for our Solicitor.

(Sal refusing to talk)

Duff: Well he won't answer.

Burrell: I'm sure it was done in compliance with the law, while, Mr Duff, we provided the resolution. There's a settlement. It's a public settlement, and then there was a statement on the record.

Duff: Mr. Burrell, you had mentioned in the last meeting that you did not know if Mr. Catrambone was involved in Center stage Entertainment and or Go Events. Isn't that correct?

Burrell: That's right.

Duff: Well, haven't you been working for Mr. Catrambone as a DJ since you were 13 years Old?

Burrell: It's well established that's how I met Gary, was with DJing. I started DJing when I was in seventh grade at middle school. Um, actually I'll pontificate, because you asked the question.

Duff: Please hold my time while you pontificate.

Burrell: I will, I will yield your time for that. Um, we had the worst school DJ's in history. So my buddy and I decided that we would DJ in seventh grade, for free and we ended up breaking the school record! And from that moment on, we actually, the teachers gave us, we borrowed a laptop, and we borrowed a speaker. From that moment on me and my buddy Jared, had a great, great business. And I met Gary um, and that's where I met Colin Rafferty, through that. Through our working together, you know, but I was never employed by any of them, any of that capacity. I mean but that's been well established for years that's how Gary eventually got me into doing this, and that's how I ran for office. But that has no bearing on my ability to govern or my ability to make any decisions. But I appreciate your question.

Duff: So uh, finishing up. I mean this is real clear. The Township of Delran literally put up a post, that you approved of, that's on your Township's site. You just said that the Communications Director is doing a great job. That you have to keep this Communications Director. You put a post up about a non-resident Mayor, who was the non-resident? Was it me?

Mayor Catrambone: I don't. I don't know.

Duff: (Heated) Come on man. You put a post up there. It was important enough for you to put a post up, and you've only had three Mayor's messages up there the whole time since you've been a mayor. That's one of them. Can you please tell us who the non-resident was in your post?

Mayor Catrambone: That's not accurate, there were way more than three messages. And I specifically did not mention the person's name.

Duff: Who's the person?

Mayor Catrambone: I'm not going to say that person's name.

Duff: Did you see Carli Lloyd's post the same day?

Mayor Catrambone: No. I don't remember.

Duff: She said there was a non-resident in Delran, "Patrick Duffy". Did you see that? You guys made it the same day!

Mayor Catrambone: I don't know. I don't remember.

Duff: Why don't you take the post down? Carli took it down.

Mayor Catrambone: All of my messages are, remain there uh, in prior messages.

Duff: But you took your page down at Center Stage Entertainment. Didn't you?

Mayor Catrambone: (nervously laughing) I, I, I am not an employee of Center Stage Entertainment.

Duff: Gary you were the first DJ, it says it in your your profile, "The first DJ at Center Stage Entertainment". Are you kidding me? Is this the Twilight Zone? That's how Jim Dunphy must have felt. By the way, I thought about it, is this the Twilight Zone here in Delran, huh? I'm zoned properly. I know I am. And all of a sudden the Mayor is showing up at my property taking pictures at the direction of the township solicitor. You paid $300,000 to a citizen that you should never have harassed. He should have been allowed to operate. That was a hidden cost. Can I ask? Is there a line item in the budget for that three hundred thousand? Because I don't think I saw it.

Burrell: Yes.

Duff: And it's for the settlement specifically? Okay, and the last just the last bit. Delran residents need 25% of registered voters to sign recall petitions for a recall. And since nobody up here is answering any questions, my suggestion is to recall them all! You recall them all. If you guys aren't willing to answer difficult questions, then why are you here, Mayor? Especially the Solicitor. That is your job is to answer questions. Legal questions about the operations of the Township. So it's sad that you won't, but I can tell you this since you won't express who the non-resident is, the non-resident was me. Isn't that correct Mr Burrell? Who else was questioning it online?

Burrell: I didn't write the post, so I don't know.

Duff: It's on the Township page though. Do you agree with the post?

Burrell: Mr. Duff the post was prepared by the Mayor's office. I did not prepare the post.

Duff: Just picture that though, remember the post said it's ridiculous to be able to question the Planning Board. When you just paid $300,000 for somebody who said that the Zoning Board was involved in racketeering, trespassing, willful taking, interference with an economic advantage, for somebody that's just trying to do business in the town. I wanted to get dressed up nice for this, because I didn't think that a lot of people would show up. But I wanted to put what happened to that man on the record, because I know when you made the settlement, all of a sudden you think everything goes away. You pay the 300k and you hope it just goes away. But what you did, you know, you admitted you showed up as property. You got picked up by the guy that was trying to scurry the property over to the Delran Historical Society. Where were you parked that day when you went to the house? When you had to get picked up by the blue Mercedes Benz? Were you just walking down the road? You live like two miles from there, so were you just walking down the road?

Mayor Catrambone: I was on the road, yeah.

Duff: Where were you parked?

Mayor Catrambone: What's the difference?

Duff: Because you were parked at Mr Buzzy's house, weren't you? Were you parked at Mr Buzzy's house? That's why Mr Buzzy picked you up, Isn't it? (Mayor just staring at me) Just admit it. It's easier that way. Thank you.

Mr. Burrell stated that before we continue with public comment he wanted to make some clarifications. When the Resolution was adopted for the settlement with Dunphy's Landscaping there was a full-page statement read into the record. Mr. Burrell stated that he commented that the agreement did not bring any joy to the Council to have to make those decisions. There were month-long conversions on the issue and it came down to a cost benefit analysis. Second, the settlement was $300,000, with $75,000 of that amount being paid through our insurance. Third, the claims alleged in the complaint were all allegations and that does not mean they would have held up in court.

Mr. Catrambone stated that nothing illegal or unethical was done in preparation and execution of the Carli Lloyd celebration event. Just because someone says it did, doesn't make it true. There are a lot of misconceptions being presented.

Delran's Dancing Mayor Turned Detective.

12-15-21

Delran Mayor Gary Catrambone was on the hot seat last night at the Township's last full council meeting of the year. Catrambone was asked why he was out taking pictures of the Dunphy Landscaping property and his responses are just priceless.

The Mayor claims that on the very brisk 39-degree, rainy day of December 9th of 2020, he was just walking down Bridgeboro Road and decided to snap some photos of 4101 Bridgeboro Road, which just happened to be the property owned by Jim Dunphy. At that time the township was defending an appeal filed by Dunphy regarding the Township's refusal to allow him to operate. Dunphy claims that when he confronted the Mayor, who was in all black and coyly taking photos of his property, the Mayor claimed that he was there taking photos at the request of Delran's own Solicitor, Sal Siciliano.

The Mayor quickly made his way across the street where he was picked up by the Vice President of the Delran Historical Society, PJ Buzzi. Just months earlier Mr Buzzi sent out dozens of fliers to residents in the area calling on them to stop Duphy's "Illegal

Operations" and asking them to show up at a June 2020 Zoning hearing and demand the Township not allow Dunphy to operate, which is exactly what they did.

The Mayor lives about 2 miles from the Dunphy property, so the thought of him just strolling down Brideboro that far away just doesn't make sense. But Buzzi, the man who picked up the Mayor, only lives about 1000 feet away from Dunphy's property. So at last night's meeting the Mayor was asked a simple question he had a lot of trouble answering...where'd he park? A question he couldn't answer.

BTW: I will be out of FB jail in the morning. Can someone pick me up across the street from Ott's?

Minutes From January 4th, 2022
Delran Council Meeting #2.

Patrick Duff, Haddon Heights resident, suggested that people making public comments should be able to be seen rather than just have their voices heard. Mr. Duff went over how his investigation of the Carli Lloyd event unfolded. He initially was told that the event cost $37,000. The cost changed at a later date to over $90,000 which didn't include public works or police overtime. Mr. Duff also stated that Mayor Catrambone mentioned that he was not employed by Center Stage Entertainment but it's been on his financial disclosure form for over a decade.

Mayor Catrambone stated that he does work for Center Stage Entertainment but he is not an employee or owner. He said he works on a gig basis.

Mr. Duff said that at the last meeting, Mayor Catrambone said he did not work for Center Stage Entertainment. Mr. Duff also stated that Mayor Catrambone took down his page on Center Stage Entertainment.

Mayor Catrambone stated that he has no control regarding the page and he does not have an interest in Center Stage Entertainment other than that they send him gigs once in a while. He stated that he never said that he doesn't work for that company. He is not an employee. He does ad hoc work.

Mr. Duff stated that makes you an employee of the company that is directly related to your brother and also to Go Events which is registered to your nephew. The Solicitor mentioned that any financial benefit to a direct relative is not legal. People want to know why your story changed?

Mayor Catrambone stated that his story didn't change. He works for Center Stage Entertainment not for Go Events.

Mr. Duff stated that the Mayor did hire Go Events for the Carli Lloyd event. Mr. Duff stated that he appreciated the ability to ask questions of individual representatives. He thought that ability might be stripped away after the resolution was passed. Mr. Duff stated that 17 days after the Dunphy application was denied, Mr. Jeney was part of a zoning hearing that approved BeeDee Associates which included Lindy Landscaping on an A1 property. Why did the Zoning Board approve this landscaping company in the same A1 zone where Dunphy's was denied?

Mr. Burrell stated that he thinks it's inappropriate for Mr. Jeney to comment on a decision that was made on behalf of a zoning board.

Mr. Jeney stated he did not feel comfortable commenting.

Mr. Duff stated to Mr. Burrell, that he stated he didn't know that the Mayor had associations with Center Stage Entertainment but he just admitted to working for them.

Mr. Burrell stated that Council knew that the Mayor worked for Center Stage Entertainment but didn't know that there was a relationship between the Mayor and Go Events. Mr. Burrell stated that he isn't happy that Go Events got paid and if Council had known there was a relationship, Council would not have approved.

Mr. Duff argued that the Mayor did know about the relationship so as a body you did have knowledge.

Mr. Burrell stated no one on the Council had knowledge of the relationship. The Mayor addressed that situation at a previous meeting and he can answer for his own actions.

Mark Oberg, resident, asked what Mr. Burrell saw as an issue with Go Events? Is it the Mayor's relationship with them?

Mr. Burrell stated that in his mind there is a difference between what is legal and what is moral or ethical. Mr. Burrell stated he doesn't think it's appropriate for anyone from the family of any member of this body to make money.

Mr. Oberg asked if the Council attends ethics training.

Mr. Burrell stated that there are various ethics training classes offered throughout the year by the Township's insurance company and the NJ League of Municipalities.

Mr. Oberg asked if Mr. Burrell felt like the Mayor should have known it was ethically wrong to allow Go Events to bid for the event. He asked what actions should be taken against the Mayor for putting Council in a bad position and breaching his code of ethics.

Mr. Burrell stated that, as the Township Solicitor explained, in his opinion, it is not a violation of the state ethics laws. Mr. Burrell stated each person has to be guided and make decisions by their own moral compass.

Mr. Oberg stated that Colin (RAC Chairman) sent emails stating that he was advised to split bids by the Solicitor. He asked if the Council has started to investigate the Mayor and Solicitor for possibly conducting things that are illegal in New Jersey. There are plenty of people asking questions about certain things that have happened over the past couple of months. Lawsuits have been filed and paid out for $300,000.00. Maybe someone should look into how they are operating as a Mayor and Solicitor. Mr. Oberg stated that they represent our Township so we become financially responsible if they aren't following the rules.

Mr. Burrell stated that the Township has retained special counsel to investigate; however, his concern is that we will pay them to find out something we already know. We have a strained budget. We are going to be deliberate and meticulous moving forward. We have an ethics counsel and we will amend the anti-nepotism ordinance to expand it.

Council President Admits Mayor Acted Unethically. 1-6-22

As the new year kicked off and Delran's Council Meetings were again restricted to Zoom, Patrick Duff and Mark Oberg had some questions about a new resolution that Council passed regarding rules of decorum. The rules seem simple, but one particular section that states that comments must be made to the "body as a whole", worried the two citizens who made the Township Committee aware of their thoughts. At one point, Council President Burrell admitted that if the Town knew the relationship that the Mayor had to Go Events, the company the town hired for $5950 for a DJ and a Band that is owned by the Mayor's own nephew, that the council would not have allowed the transaction to happen.

In a shocking turn of events, just a couple hours after the two meetings below concluded, Delran's Mayor Gary Catrambone put out a statement calling on the state to investigate himself and the actions of the Township regarding the Carli Lloyd event. The statement reads as if the Mayor has been the victim of a smear campaign against the whole town and everyone in it. The Mayor is claiming that false narratives and unfounded accusations have been levied on Social Media, yet none of the difficult questions that have been asked in regards to the planning of the Carli Lloyd event have ever been properly explained.

Why did the Solicitor tell Colin Rafferty that the quotes must be separated? Why did the Town spend $61,500 on a stage and video equipment? Why did the Mayor hire his Nephew's company? Why weren't bids sought for contracts that obviously were above the bidding threshold? While it is important that these questions are answered and it's very noble of the Mayor to call for the NJ Comptroller to investigate his and the Townships actions regarding the Carli Party, the real call needs to go to the Attorney General to investigate what the Mayor and certain Township officials did to Dunphy's Landscaping.

Several weeks ago the Council President Tyler Burrell and the Delran's Solicitor both made public proclamations that if there were any allegations of crimes made to the Council, that they would call the Attorney General themselves and demand for an investigation. Yet as you will hear from the questions asked of the Council below, that has still yet to happen. So, 23 allegations were made against the Mayor and the Town's Zoning Board. Those allegations included RICO violations, Abuse of Power, Trespassing, interference with an economic advantage and over a dozen more.

These are serious allegations of criminal activity that make the bid splitting and conflicts of interest from the Carli Party look like tiddly-winks. The citizens of the Township deserve for the Council President and the Solicitor to follow through on their promise to report the criminal allegations to the proper authorities, if they refuse to do so, that just makes them look like an accessory.

CHAPTER 7
Hit Blogs & Lawsuits

Things really began to heat up after I released the information about the Dunphy settlement, and the council was now implementing new rules. These new rules were coined by some as "The Duff Rules", because they now will only allow for five minutes per speaker, because otherwise I would have continued deposing them for 20 plus minutes. The council also had now decided that they needed to switch back to virtual meetings due to COVID even though there was no legitimate reason to do so at that time. But little did they know that I was grateful, because it saved me a 20 minute drive both ways to attend the meetings.

Speaking of driving, the thought of Mayor Catrambone just walking down Bridgeboro Road, some two miles away from his house, just didn't make sense. But what did make sense is if the Mayor parked 1,000 feet away from the direction that he was walking from at the Vice President of the Delran Historical Society's house, P.J. Buzzi, another young recruit of Gary Cat. Now the Mayor could have just walked back to Buzzi's house, but that would have given away where he parked, and Buzzi had already been on a campaign of smearing the landscaping company, so if Gary Cat went back to his house he'd have given up their connection. Which he did anyway when Buzzi picked him up while he was hiding in the bank on the corner. So I guess his walk was over?

When a government entity such as Delran refuses to release public information through an OPRA request, the requester has two choices; Accept it and say nothing, which I never recommend, or send an email challenging the refusal or redactions and ask for an internal review, which you should do on any denial you believe is unlawful. If they still refuse you can either file a complaint with the Government Records Council, or file a lawsuit in Superior Court, which at this point in the battle I was undefeated in eight OPRA denial cases.

I have used my attorney CJ Griffin now in a dozen or more cases, all of them being victorious, with one that is currently being heard in front of the NJ Appellate Division court. CJ and her associates have spent well over one hundred hours on my cases, yet I have never paid them a dime because the government entity does. OPRA cases come with a legal term that's called fee shifting, which simply means the defendant pays the legal bills if the plaintiff is victorious. This is supposed to give government entities more of an incentive to follow the OPRA laws. Only it's not their money so they just don't seem to give a shit if they get sued.

I knew the whole damn Carli party was just one big campaign event for Phil Murphy that Delran taxpayers paid for. Phil's wife Tammy was even in attendance and blessed the stage, as did her now opponent for a U.S. Senate slot, Congressman Andy Kim, along with a dozen other high ranking Democrats. However not one Republican politician was invited to the Lloyd party.

Obtaining the video wasn't going to be easy though, because the Township was fighting me tooth and nail on releasing it to me. The Township was claiming that they could not release video of the event because children were in the videos. But that's just silly, especially considering the Township had already shared images of those same children with several media outlets with no regard, including the NY Times, and the event was also featured on several local TV news outlets.

When I requested those same photos that I knew were already

sent to other media outlets without any redactions, Delran responded with the same images, only with all of the kids' faces blacked out. Now remember, this was a public event, one that was on the news, in magazines, and surely had no expectation of privacy, so why were they stonewalling?

I can tell you from the case law that Council President Burrell quoted that they were trying to paint me as some sort of pedophile just for asking for the videos of the party, because the case they quoted as their legal justification had to do with a child molestor, and not publicly held records as Burrell falsely claimed. The troll army also joined in by asking in FB groups why I would want pictures of little kids? Also trying to infer I wanted the video of Carli Lloyd's retirement party for some twisted sexual reason having to do with the children, when they all knew that not to be the case. The anonymous blogger also was pushing the same narrative because of the OPRA request I sent to the Bridge Commission, claiming that I was some type of "sicko" just because I made a request for information on the suicide on one of the bridges the Commission controlled.

The political climate was boiling over at this point, and the Delran Mayor had yet to actually explain himself. But as you will read below, he doesn't do a very good job when he tries.

Controversial Carli Video To Be Discussed At Tonight's Council Meeting. 1-18-22

Delran Township's Council will meet tonight at 7 pm via ZOOM for the first time since Delran's Council President, Tyler Burrell, called out Mayor Gary Catrambone for his unethical behavior by the town hiring of his own nephew's company to provide a DJ and band at a cost of $5,950 for the Carli Lloyd Retirement Celebration.

At the last Council meeting the Council President said that if the Council had known that the Mayor's nephew owned Go Events, they would have never hired that company. Even though Council President Burrell clearly stated he believed the Mayor acted unethically in the hiring of his own nephew, Mayor Gary Catrambone released his own statement claiming that he not only did nothing wrong, conveniently leaving out the fact that it was the Council President that had already stated so on the record, but he also called for himself to be investigated.

That statement put out by Mayor Gary Catrambone was most likely penned by Wendy Mitchell, the controversial Communications Director who has her job also on the line tonight as Council discusses the new contract for Delran's newest position, Delran's Communications Director, a job that Mayor Catrambone himself lobbied for last year to be added to Delran's payroll.

The contract in 2021 that was made for communications director was made between the Township of Delran and WLMitchell Consulting without ever going to a public bid, a company that does not actually exist. Even though the Town has a contract with WLMitchell Consulting, they accepted a business registration certificate and W9 from Wendy Mitchell as an individual and required no proof of business insurance, even though Wendy was allegedly acting as an outside contractor.

The Council will also be discussing the release of an OPRA request that Rabble Rouser Media filed with Delran Township for the release of the videos taken and paid for by Delran's taxpayers of the Carli Lloyd Retirement Party. While the Township freely shared images of the event and all of it's participants with local and national media, that included dozens of children faces, they are refusing to share the videos taken of the Carli Lloyd party by claiming that the faces of the children that attended the event would need to be redacted and that Rabble Rouser Media would have to pay for the blurring of the kids faces, which could cost big money.

Why is the Township being so resistant to sharing the videos? Is it that they want to blur the kids' faces to protect the identities that the Town already shared with local and national media? Or is it that they want to hide the fact that the party was a bust and blur the faces of the dozens of politicians who showed up to a party that the Mayor claimed would be attended by thousands, yet only a couple hundred, mostly children, attended.

Will the Mayor respond tonight to the Council President's allegations that he acted unethically in hiring his nephew? Will the Township again hire Wendy Mitchell as the Communications Director? Will the Council approve the release of the Carli Party video? Well you better get your favorite snack and beverage ready and tune in tonight at 7 pm HERE to find out!

Minutes From January 18th, 2022 Delran Council Meeting.

Patrick Duff asked Ms. McPeak (Solicitor filling in for Mr Siciliano) if she is aware that there were emails sent to news sources by Delran Township that included pictures of children at the Carli Lloyd event. He argued that there is no reason for the video to be redacted when pictures were already shared by the Township.

Ms. McPeak explained she can't change what has happened but moving forward the municipality is going to have to abide by OPRA and redact personal identifiers.

Mr. Duff asked for case law on this subject.

Mr. Burrell referenced Doe vs. Poritz, Recorder 142 NJ 1, Page 8, published in 1995 which involved an OPRA request and videos.

Mr. Duff stated that he will be suing Delran Township. He also remarked that while the mayor believes that he did not act unethically regarding the hiring of Go Events for the Carli

Lloyd Event, the Council President stated that the mayor did act unethically.

Mr. Catrambone responded that the Council President stated there was a difference in ethics, not that anything was done unethically.

Mr. Duff explained that the reason Delran is not releasing the video is because the event was not successful. Mr. Duff also asked Mr. Burrell about the Mayor taking pictures of the Dunphy property.

Mr. Burrell stated he does not know exactly what happened and he isn't going to comment. Mr. Catrambone explained it was not unethical to take pictures of the property.

Councilman Tom Lyon made a motion to close the public comment, seconded by Mr. Jeney. All were in favor; the motion was approved.

Mr. Burrell then stressed that while there may have been issues with redacting in the past, moving forward, we have to take the advice of our Solicitor's Office. It has nothing to do with trying to prevent the video from being released.

Minutes From January 25th, 2022 Delran Council Meeting.

Mr. Catrambone reported that last week he became aware of a new blog that seemed to be focusing on one individual. While he fundamentally disagrees with the narrative on the first blog as the manipulation of facts during Council meetings over the last few months has been something we are all dealing with. Mr. Catrambone stated that he does not condone this new blog's nonsense in any way. He does not know the motivation behind the person doing this but we will not be dragged into a blog war. This behavior only further distracts from the work we have to do. This blog, if created by a Delran resident, is not helping.

Mr. Catrambone stated that he wanted to update the residents that he recently submitted a letter to the Local Finance Board and is also waiting on a response from the Comptroller's Office on the audit he requested.

Mr. Burrell echoed the comments from the Mayor related to the recent blog and stated that we need to start acting like adults.

Mr. Gabor (resident) stated both the Mayor and Council President reference a blog but did not provide a name. Mr. Gabor stated that he has an issue with the Government trying to silence someone on the web and asked if they could provide the name of the blog.

Mr. Burrell stated that he doesn't have the name of the blog but it is something to the effect of sunshine disinfects. The blog makes allegations that a certain person faked cancer and he feels that is inappropriate. Everyone has free speech but it doesn't mean we have to agree.

Mr. Gabor asked what the point of mentioning the blog was, if they weren't going to give the name.

Mr. Catrambone stated that this blog was against an individual not at the Township but he felt it was not helping the dialogue or interaction we are trying to have. He is not going to promote the blog because he doesn't agree with what it says.

Patrick Duff, stated that the blog the Mayor and Council mentioned is a blog that is talking about him and stating he faked his cancer and other defamatory things against him. He can assure everyone that he is not faking his cancer.

Mr. Duff asked if there is any stipulation in the insurance that caused the Township not to go through the insurance company with regards to Dunphy's because the deductible was only $75,000. Mr. Duff stated that Dunphy's never filed a tort claim or a demand letter with the Township yet the Township settled for $300,000. The big issue with that is the Township is settling on illegal advice that the Solicitor gave the Mayor and they all signed off on the settlement. Mr. Duff asked if the Council voted on the payout.

Mr. Burrell stated that there was a Resolution and vote.

Mr. Duff asked if Council thinks it's a problem that the individuals that committed the illegal and unethical acts were the ones to negotiate the settlement. He is asking that the Council ask the Attorney General for an investigation.

Mr. Burrell stated that there was a demand letter issued to the Township. The goal was to keep this out of litigation. Allegations are not facts until proven.

Minutes From February 1st, 2022 Delran Council Meeting.

Patrick Duff, Haddon Heights resident, stated that the Township has put out various statements and he is wondering when a statement is read at a Township meeting, is it always posted online.

Mr. Burrell stated that normally they are all posted. It is an administrative function.

Mr. Duff asked if they remember any statements that were read and not posted for the public.

Mr. Burrell stated that he believes almost every statement is posted.

Mr. Duff stated that the only statement he can identify that has not been posted online, is the statement read into the record regarding the Dunphy settlement, which showed a $300,000 settlement.

Mr. Burrell stated that he believed it was posted online but he did prepare a statement and read it into the record at the public meeting.

Mr. Duff stated that it was not posted online.

Mr. Duff asked the Mayor if he believes that his post online about Mr. Duff sparked the hit blog against him.

Mayor Catrambone stated that he has no idea what sparked that blog.

Mr. Duff stated that what Ms. Littleton was trying to get at during her comments were that both Mr. Jeney and Mr. Smith were on the Zoning Board and voted against the Dunphy application. Then they both voted for the settlement as members of Council. Mr. Duff stated that they should have recused themselves and he believes their votes should be voided.

Mr. Duff stated that the Township should have gone through the insurance company. Mr. Duff stated that he spoke with the JIF and they stated that when a claim is received the insurance provider thoroughly investigates the allegations contained within the complaint. If the investigation determines that the actions of those involved were illegal or resulted from willful misconduct of their role within the municipality, coverage can and will be denied. So basically, what they were saying is that if the claims presented by Dunphy's were found to be true, the insurance company would not have covered the claims. Mr. Duff stated that he would like to call for an investigation into the fact that Delran didn't print Dunphy's statement online and it was a cover up to not report it to the insurance company.

Mr. Burrell stated that he can not speak to why the statement was not posted on the website.

Mayor Catrambone stated that the other statements Mr. Duff was referring to were posted in the Mayor's Message. The statement on the Dunphy's settlement was read into the record at a public meeting.

Mr. Siciliano stated that the self-serving statement by Mr. Duff was filled with so many inaccuracies and incorrect assumptions and conclusions. He does not feel that it is appropriate to attempt to answer those falsehoods.

Mr. Burrell stated that at no point was this an attempt to cover anything up, in fact if it was there would not have been such an extensive statement read into the record.

(Resident) Tony Egan stated that he would like to yield his time to Mr. Duff.

Mr. Siciliano stated that five minutes are allotted per speaker. He cannot yield or assign his time.

Mr. Egan asked what Mr. Siciliano has to hide since he doesn't want to speak with Mr. Duff.

Mr. Siciliano stated that he has nothing to hide.

Mark Oberg, (resident) stated that Council has the opportunity to go to the insurance company when any type of legal action is filed against the Township. Mr. Oberg asked how long the Township waited to notify the insurance company that there was the potential for a lawsuit to be filed by Dunphy's.

Mr. Burrell stated that he does not have that information in front of him tonight.

Mr. Oberg stated that it was not immediately, and probably even after the settlement.

Mr. Siciliano stated that is not correct. There is nothing in the record to indicate that it wasn't timely or that it was after the settlement.

Mr. Oberg asked if Mr. Siciliano will apologize on the record if it is found to have been after the settlement. There were two individuals that were named in the complaint that voted for the settlement and should have recused themselves. It is a matter of ethics as someone named in the suit should not be negotiating the settlement.

(Resident) Mrs. Morgan stated she moved here and it just appears that everything is ridden with scandal. She sees things on Facebook and now she is hearing about these lawsuits and she feels that there is a lot of mistrust. If there is anyone that can speak to how they plan to rebuild that trust.

Mr. Burrell stated that he appreciates her concern and understands where she is coming from. He cannot change the minds of the people. The only thing that Council can do is continue to provide the services that the residents want and continue to do the work that they do to make the community a better place.

Mr. Lyon made a motion to close the meeting to the public, seconded by Mr. Smith. All were in favor; the motion was approved.

Mayor Catrambone stated that he has been holding back his comments. The accusations that have been made and not even issues anymore yet continue to be discussed. Specifically, one of the accusers was told back in December that there were no violations of ethics by the Department of Community Affairs regarding the handling of the contracts for the Carli Lloyd event but there is a refusal to acknowledge that truth. At no point was that information shared with the residents but instead individuals continue to ask the same questions and state incorrect information in blogs and in meetings even though the answers have been provided. The other thing that is really important is the cost to the Township for all of this above and beyond the stress to the Township employees and staff. This also cost the Township a significant amount financially in terms of the numerous OPRA requests we have received. This all started with a question about the sponsorship of the fireworks, which was about $12,000. As of right now, the total cost for the OPRA requests we have received from October through December have cost the Township taxpayers $20,973.71. Unfortunately,there doesn't appear to be an end in sight. The event is not, as accused, a political or campaign event. No money was given to anyone running for office nor collected for any candidate. The first lady of NJ attended the event because she and the Governor are co-owners of the Gotham Football Club as well as personal friends of Carli Lloyd. Mr. Catrambone reminded everyone that Dunphy's litigation is settled. The settlement does not indicate any fault. If we continue to drag this on it should have cost the Township double in legal fees. At the advice of legal, we evaluated the cost to fight the case and determined it would be fiscally more responsible to settle. Mr. Catrambone stated that he never trespassed on the property. He took the photos from the street. No allegations were ever filed, this was just the threat of a lawsuit. Mr. Catrambone stated that he would be happy to answer any legitimate questions by residents.

CHAPTER 8

So Long Sal.

It's funny that Mayor Gary Cat continually said he was willing to answer any legitimate questions by residents, as if the fact that I was not a current resident made my questions any less legitimate. Even if my questions were voided due to my lack of residency, actual residents like Mark Oberg and Barbara Littleton were also asking the same questions of the mayor, Council, and Solicitor "Don't call me Sal" Siciliano, yet they all still refused to answer.

In the legal profession there is a term that is used when a lawyer admits that they screwed up on their client's case called "falling on the sword". It's normally done to avoid malpractice suits, or for well connected people who pulled some strings to get out of trouble, but either way it's something attorneys do not like to do as it could affect their law license. At this point so much was pointing at Sal for offering bad legal advice that one would think he'd fall on the sword and just walk away, but he was holding strong and getting ready to release a memo the Mayor promised to the citizens that was finally going to answer the difficult questions I had posed.

These questions now included serious allegations of criminal behavior, and how that behavior was covered up by the same parties who committed the legally questionable acts, such as Lynn Jeney. Prior to Lynn becoming a Council member, he was the President of the same Zoning Board that arbitrarily denied Dunphy's variance. So it was clear that he should have recused himself from voting on the Dunphy settlement, but he didn't.

At this point you had the Mayor claiming Sal told him to go take pictures of Dunphy's property, and Jeney claiming that Sal told him he didn't need to recuse himself from the settlement vote. But without me asking questions when I did, none of it would have been known to the public. The exposure of these issues was also now making it difficult for the Mayor's troll army to have anything to say, but they were still trying.

Many trolls like to use fake names to do their dirty work, but since these are not the smartest beings on the planet, they always leave some crumbs behind for me to find. Most of these trolls are infected with a little bit of power afforded to them by the Mayor, and they'll do anything to hold on to their little slice of the power pie. So I always check to see who the Mayor appointed to the Planning and Zoning boards, local committees such as the Recreation Committee, as well as get a current list of the municipalities Democratic and Republican Committee members, which in most cases is run by the head idiot in charge.

Delran's Democratic Committee is no different, it's headed by DJ Gary Cat himself, and has been for decades. When you step out of line like Burrell did, it's off with your head and you are replaced, just as Burrell was replaced by Assemblyman Herb Conway on Delran's Committee. Most people have never even heard of such a committee, yet these small groups of people hold the power of selecting the candidates that run office. They are the gatekeepers you might say, and that power can be infectious.

One such troll from Delran used the fake name "Henry Dubya", and he had an awful lot of bad things to say about me, that was until I identified him as a member of not only the Town's committee, but he was also a founding member of the same Historical Society that was trying to hijack Dunphy for his property, so he was in on the cover up.

Once I identified him and let him know that he was going to be famous in Town the next day when he was the feature of my new article, he literally begged for mercy. He not only begged me, but he also begged the moderator of the Delran Resident's Official FaceBook page, my now friend Daniel Brennan.

Now I must take a minute to say that if it weren't for Daniel Brennan and his refusal to ban me from his FaceBook group, even though dozens of people requested that he do so, none of this would have been possible. Access to the masses is a must for this type of work. Without access to those 8,500 members on the FaceBook page, my stories would have fallen flat. In just the four months up until this point of writing stories about Delran, and publishing them locally on Rabble Rouser, my site had close to 60,000 views already.

Daniel contacted me and asked me to do him the favor of not outing "Dubya" for who he really was, and said that "Dubya" promised to never stick his nose in my business again, to which I agreed. I am sure that as "Henry Dubya" reads this he is thanking his lucky stars that Daniel stepped in on his behalf.

You see, as I said previously Daniel and I shared a common enemy, Wendy Mitchell, who had viciously come after Daniel in the past. He loved to watch from the sidelines as I picked her apart, so he gave me the freedom to say what I wanted other than this one request, which I thought was more than fair.

The tension at this point in Delran politics had never been higher, with the council admittedly hamstrung from my investigations, and Sal refusing to answer questions. Now the Mayor was claiming that "Don't call me Sal" was ready to answer those difficult questions, but as you will see, that is something that never happened.

Minutes From February 8th, 2021 Council Meeting.

Mr. Lyon stated that the Council is not corrupt and none of its members have done anything wrong. He also believes that the Mayor has done nothing illegal and trusts that he has done nothing wrong. Mr. Lyon believes that there is a self-serving, disingenuous person that does not care about Delran or the taxpayers. Instead, he cares about promoting himself and making money through potential lawsuits. His behavior and that of his lackey was pathetic. That being said, this person has asked pertinent questions that have either not been completely answered or ignored. The Mayor should have explained what happened and the sequence of those events. Mr. Siciliano should have stated why, in his opinion, there were no legal missteps. I'm frustrated by the lack of answers by certain individuals on the Township side but truly believe that this is not a corrupt Council.

Mr. Burrell stated that he has waited for people twice his age to make things right but they haven't. The Mayor can and must answer the questions for his own conduct. Council cannot be held to the fire for someone else's conduct. Local government is where we are the closest we can be to our elected officials. The Township and Council have been consumed by one individual who is repeatedly litigating the conduct of one person. It has crippled the structure of the Township to get anything done. It is extremely frustrating and embarrassing. The Council is trying its best to do the job that we need to do. Mr. Burrell stated that he grew up in Delran and wants to stay here. This is the Township that he loves and he wants to make it a better place. He is trying very hard to get things accomplished but he will not answer for someone else. Mr. Burrell said that Council will not ask for the Mayor's resignation but stresses that the Mayor needs to do what is right for the Township.

Mr. Burrell then stated that he is deeply concerned about the quality of our legal representation. He is losing faith, trust and confidence in the advice received from Mr. Siciliano. Mr. Siciliano has been asked to articulate his reasoning to the public and Council and that has not happened. Mr. Burrell then asked for the resignation of the solicitor's office. He explained that it was nothing personal but was for the greater good of the Township. If a resignation is not received, Council will use its legislative authority under the Township Code and Title 40. Mr. Burrell asked Council to work on a closed session item to discuss potential litigation matters.

(Resident) Ms. Littleton congratulated Mr. Lyon on some of the comments he made. She did want to stress that she doesn't necessarily agree that the person Mr. Lyon was speaking of said things for his own personal gain. He has brought things to our attention, causing us to get involved in the Township. Everyone should be appreciative of what he has found.

Ms. Littleton stated that, regardless of the advice they received, she felt that it was a conflict of interest for Mr. Jeney and Mr. Smith to vote on the Dunphy case. She explained that they were both on the Zoning Board initially and then voted on the settlement case also. Ms. Littleton applauded Mr. Burrell on his comments. She stated that it is very frustrating that Mr. Siciliano refused to give answers to the taxpayers. The Mayor is the least transparent person she has ever seen. Ms. Littleton explained that the Mayor should have been honest about his mistakes. Ms. Littleton asked whether the Township notified the insurance company when Dunphy filed an appeal.

Mr. Siciliano explained that this is a question for Jeff Hatcher who was the JIF representative at the time.

Ms. Littleton announced she has been in touch with the insurance company who stated that they were not notified. The Township paid legal costs that the insurance company would have paid if they had been notified.

Mr. Joyce stated that he admired the speeches that Mr. Burrell and Mr. Lyon gave this evening. He then asked whether the

Mayor reported his actions to state agencies.

Mr. Catrambone said that he has done that. He also stated that along the lines of transparency, Mr. Duff received a response from the DCA on December 2nd. The response outlined that Delran Township has a dedication by rider approval for donations for special events. The retirement event would be considered a special event. Also, the local public contracts law does not prohibit using vendors that are related to local officials. Additionally, the Delran quote threshold is $6,600 so no other quotes were required for this service. Mr. Catrambone did not realize at the time that the agent used to book the entertainment had outsourced that job to an agency owned by the Mayor's relative, to get a better price. They will not be using them again in the future but it was not illegal to hire them for the event.

Mr. Duff proclaimed that in regard to the Dunphy statement, the minutes don't reflect the statement that was made. Mr. Duff stated that he is not doing this for financial gain. He also explained that there was no clear response to what the Carli Lloyd event cost. By not asking for the resignation of Mr. Catrambone, you still have the head of the beast who is a liability to the town.

Ms. Mitchell stated that due to the occurrences over the last few months, this is the first time that she can remember when Council, the Mayor and Township professionals needed a police escort to their cars after public meetings. She also stated that she could not bring her five- year-old son to Delran's WinterFest because his picture was posted on Mr. Duff's blog and the Police Department and Council determined that it was probably unsafe to bring him to the event.

Delran Council President Asks Solicitor To Resign.

Nearly 5 months after the drama known as the Delran Debacle

began, Delran's Council President Tyler Burrell, the 25 year old newly minted lawyer, decided enough was enough and asked the Township's Solicitor, Sal Siciliano, to resign for the good of the Delran community. If you have been paying attention over these last couple of months you'd know that Sal has been one of the biggest stars of the Debacle, in fact, without his wonderful legal advice most of this would not have happened. So, in a sense, I have to thank Sal, it's solicitors like him who make the bad case law that activists hang our hats on, such is about to happen over the Carli Lloyd video the Township claims they cannot share.

Imagine, they took hours of video of the event, video that they claim they cannot share due to privacy issues...so why take the video at all? Why spend thousands to have professional video cameras shoot the event if the footage itself cannot be shared? The answer is, that it can be but certain people do not want it released because it will show the event was a bust. The Mayor claimed thousands showed up, I say not a chance. At the very beginning of this I wrote that Carli's retirement party ironically just might have been for the Mayor, which looks to be coming true.

On October 19th the Mayor put out a message about the nonresident who was claiming bribery and coercion were taking place regarding a variance, something that I never claimed. I originally asked for an apology, to remove the message, and to allow for free speech on the Facebook pages of the Mayor and the Township. That offer was laughed at by the Mayor, an action that I gave fair warning to. I let him know that over the years I have acquired a very particular set of skills that make me a nightmare for people like the Mayor, but he didn't listen.

Minutes From February 22nd,

2022 Council Meeting.

Mr. Catrambone thanked the interim solicitor, Ms. Fahey, for jumping in at a moment's notice earlier this afternoon so we could have this meeting. She will also help us get through the process of appointing the next Township solicitor.

Mr. Jeney spoke out on some issues that the Township government has been facing in recent months. He explained that he is dissatisfied with the way that the issues have been handled by the Mayor. Clear, succinct responses would have been better than no responses. That being said, the state, the Mayor and the Township attorney have all reported that there was no wrongdoing. We must move forward. Mr. Jeney discussed how disturbing it is to be escorted by police after meetings due to aggressive and threatening behavior by some individuals. Mr. Jeney reported that the false and misleading narrative was created by an individual to achieve notoriety and to possibly obtain money from the Township and that the individual has done this before in other municipalities. As far as the Dunphy settlement, Mr. Jeney and Mr. Smith were advised by counsel that recusing themselves was not necessary. They went on to vote honestly and with integrity. Mr. Jeney explained the best interest of Delran is always his priority and he requests an apology from anyone stating false and malicious information.

Mr. Burrell thanked Mr. Siciliano, former solicitor, for his service to the township and for moving on peacefully.

Ms. Littleton thanked the people who worked on the grants for the Township. She explained that she submits OPRA requests to validate Council and the Mayor's responses. Ms. Littleton stated that she doesn't believe Council and the Mayor know what transparency means. She asked the mayor if he received a response from the state ethics committee.

Mr. Catrambone explained that he did not but Mr. Duff received one for his request.

Ms. Littleton stated that the Mayor has proclaimed there is a misrepresentation of facts but she feels that the Mayor has misrepresented the facts. She stated that there were two separate requests that Mr. Duff made to the State Department of Community Affairs. They reported there was no violation on the first request but after Mr. Duff provided more explanation in his second request, the state pointed Mr. Duff to the source documents where he could find the answers himself. She proceeded to explain that when Mr. Duff asked for the cost of the Carli Lloyd event he received different responses. Ms. Littleton also reported that the Mayor trespassed on Dunphy's property and she can prove it.

Mr. Burrell explained about the changing numbers regarding the Carli Lloyd event. The billing process is lengthy. At the end of the event, not all of the costs have been processed yet. There was no malicious intent.

Mr. Egan questioned Mr. Jeney's statement regarding police escorts to vehicles. Mr. Egan asked if there was a reason that there was a police presence at the meeting.

Mr. Jeney explained that he and Mr. Lyon were aggressively approached by Mr. Duff's posse. He and Mr. Lyon walked away but the posse followed him until Mr. Duff pulled them back. Mr. Jeney remarked that a police escort probably wasn't necessary but the chief of police stated he didn't want to see anything happen in his jurisdiction.

Mr. Egan reported that someone who has voiced their opinion in these meetings had their tires slashed and someone else received a threat of being shot in the face. Mr. Egan asked when Wendy Mitchell obtained her insurance for her Communications Director position.

Mr. Catrambone stated he didn't know but he could get that information.

Mr. Egan informed him that it was January 17, 2022 so she went a year as the Communications Director without insurance.

Mr. Catrambone explained that it wasn't requested initially but when it was requested she provided the insurance.

Mr. Egan asked if it was Mr. Bellina's job to check up on contractors that work for the township. Mr. Bellina stated that it was.

Mr. Egan stated that Mr. Duff requested the video for the Carli Lloyd event but was told that the faces of the minors in it would have to be redacted. He asked if that was the case, why is Wendy Mitchell posting the pictures of the minors on the Delran 2.0 website.

Mr. Catrambone explained that the only Delran government pages are the official website and the Facebook page. What Ms. Mitchell does in her own time is her own time.

Mr. Duff stated that Mr. Lyon accused him of making money from OPRA lawsuits but Mr. Duff informed that he has never made money from OPRA lawsuits. Mr. Duff also stated that Mr. Jeney accused him of presenting facts that were false. Mr. Duff explained that the facts he was presenting were from answers received from a variety of OPRA requests.

Mr. Jeney stated that Mr. Duff revealed that he earned $7,000 from suing another township.

Mr. Duff denied that. Mr. Duff then asked for the memo that the Township Solicitor was going to produce explaining various issues. He also asked whether the Mayor offered to buy the Dunphy property after the Zoning Board refused the variance. Mr. Duff informed everyone that he has filed a lawsuit against Delran Township regarding the Carli Lloyd video. Mr. Duff also wants to know why the Solicitor resigned. In addition to that, he accused Delran Township of insurance fraud.

Mr. Burrell explained that the Township considered buying the Dunphy property early on but was unable to do that for various reasons. After the zoning hearing there was an appeal and the Township Solicitor reached out to Dunphy's to get an update on the sale status. It is not uncommon for township's to do this. Sometimes properties go through the zoning process and are approved, only to ask the township if they are interested in purchasing the land because a business deal has fallen through.

Mr. Catrambone thanked Mr. Burrell for filling in the details regarding Dunphy's. He also stated that he didn't know that Mr. Siciliano, the former Delran Solicitor, was going to resign prior to him doing so. He doesn't have an answer as to why he resigned but as soon as he gets an answer, he will share it.

Scott Ducko (Duff's Side Kick) stated that last week the Council President asked the Solicitor and, indirectly, the Mayor, to resign. Is this still his position?

Mr. Burrell stated he is glad that the Solicitor did the right thing for the Township so we can move forward and he is not going to relitigate his past comments.

Mr. Ducko asked if there was a credible threat regarding Wendy Mitchell's son attending the Winter Festival.

Mr. Burrell stated that he doesn't speak for Ms. Mitchell.

Mr. Ducko stated that he knew Mr. Lyon was referring to him when he mentioned Mr. Duff's "lackey." He explained that he and Mr. Duff did nothing threatening in regards to the exchange between them and Mr. Jeney and Mr. Lyon. He then accused Mr. Jeney and Mr. Lyon of behaving in a threatening manner towards him. Mr. Ducko also suggested that the Mayor resign.

Delran Tried To Buy Dunphy Property

After Illegally Denying Variance.

When 4101 Bridgeboro Road came up for sale in 2019, several parties showed interest in purchasing the property, which included Delran's former Council President and current Mayor, Gary Catrambone, as well as Dunphy Landscaping. Catrambone admitted that the town had an interest in buying the property so they could preserve open space and also to give a home to the Delran Historical Society, an organization that Catrambone helped found over a decade ago. The property at 4101 Bridgeboro Road was once owned by the Garwood Family, which included Delran's first Mayor, Robert F. Garwood, giving it the historical significance that would make a great home for any Historical Society.

The Township couldn't purchase the property right away though, and the owner instead sold it to 4101 Bridgeboro Road LLC in October of 2019, to be used as the home of Dunphy's Landscaping. 4101 Bridgeboro Road had significance to Dunphy as well, especially considering that it was in the same A1 zone that four other landscaping companies existed in, so Dunphy thought it was a perfect home for his business.

Delran originally issued a permit to Dunphy Landscaping to operate, but something changed about two weeks later when the Township began to demand that Dunphy needed to file paperwork with the township that was not being required of any of the four other companies that had been operating in the same zone for years, one even being directly across the street from the 4101 Bridgeboro Road location.

Even though the things being demanded of Dunphy were not being demanded of others, Dunphy, through his attorney, tried to comply. Yet in January, 2020 the Township's Zoning Officer Ted Reimel pulled Dunphy's permits. When Dunphy asked why he was doing so, Reimel replied that "He doesn't want to get in the middle of it" and that "I only have five years left", which left Dunphy confused. When Reimel pulled Dunphy's permit, he rendered the property useless, and the Township even made him clear all of his own equipment from the property.

Dunphy filed for a variance that was finally heard on June 30th of 2020, at a hearing where only one Township official spoke, now Council Person and Former Zoning Board member, Lynn Jenney. Along with Jenney speaking, two of the detractors to speak were PJ Buzzi Jr, and Julie Weimer, who both live close to 4101 Bridgeboro Road. PJ Buzzi Jr is the VP of the Delran Historical Society, which is the same organization that Catrambone founded and also the one that was set to benefit if the Township acquired 4101 Bridgeboro Road as their new home. Prior to the hearing Buzzi submitted a 14 page letter to the Zoning Board and he had also distributed fliers to the neighborhood calling Dunphy's Landscaping an "illegal business" and asking for people to come out and fight against them.

Even though the evidence that was submitted by Dunphy's attorney's was more than enough to overturn the decision to pull their permits and grant the variance, the Zoning Board, headed by Lynn Jenney, denied the variance on the grounds that landscaping companies were not a permitted use in the A1 zone. Now remember, at this point four other landscaping companies were operating in the same A1 zone, so how could Jenney claim it was not a permitted use? To add insult to injury, just 17 days after Delran's Zoning Board denied Dunphy's variance on the grounds that landscaping companies were not authorized to operate in that zone, the Delran Zoning Board, headed by Lynn Jenney, approved another landscaping company to operate in the same A1 zone.

At this point Dunphy's property had been useless to him for almost a year, so in a last ditch effort, he filed an appeal of the variance hearing in Burlington County Superior Court on September 1st of 2020. The representatives from the Town's insurance company say that this is the point where they should have alerted the insurer, but they failed to do so, resulting in the later denial of the claim. The week after Dunphy filed his appeal, the Delran Township Council, headed by then Council President Gary Catrambone, had a closed session meeting to discuss the acquisition of a property in town. When a citizen asked which property was being considered, Catrambone refused to say the address, but from emails garnered in OPRA requests it was discovered that the property that they were discussing acquiring was in fact Dunphy's property. Just a couple of days later the Township offered to buy Dunphy's property, the same property that the Zoning Board had rendered useless, in an offer they thought Dunphy couldn't refuse, but he did.

That November of 2020 Catrambone was elected as Mayor and his running mate Lynn Jenney was elected to Town Council, which meant Jenney had to resign his position on the Zoning Board. Just a month later, as Dunphy's appeal was winding its way through the courts and survived several motions to attempt to have the case dismissed, Mayor elect Catrambone was caught trespassing on Dunphy's property taking pictures to turn into the court to try and hurt Dunphy's chance of appeal. When he was confronted, Dunphy alleged that Catrambone claimed that he was there to take pictures at the request of the Township's Solicitor Sal Siciliano. Catrambone quickly walked away and walked across the street, where he was picked up by the VP of the Delran Historical Society, PJ Buzzi.

At this point, Dunphy wanted to learn more of what was happening to him, so he made a call to the woman he purchased the property from, Kitty Newman. Dunphy alleges that Newman told him that when she told Catrambone that she was thinking of selling the property to Dunphy, Catrambone replied that Dunphy would never get a permit to operate and she let Dunphy know about Catrambone's interest to buy the property, something that up until this point, Dunphy had no idea of. Superior Court Judge Jeanne Covert heard the appeal of the variance on January 14th of 2021, ruling that the Township illegally denied Dunphy's variance and acted in a completely arbitrary and capricious manner in doing so, overturning the denial of the variance.

Delran's new council and Mayor met just two weeks later and held a closed session meeting to discuss "litigation regarding 4101 Bridgeboro Road". On February 2nd Delran again held a meeting to discuss "Litigation Settlement Discussions-4101 Bridgeboro Road", which shows pretty clearly that the town was already in discussions with Dunphy's attorney's regarding the pending lawsuit that was about to be filed, yet that is not the story the Township told the insurance company.

The insurance company says that the Township claims that they were first alerted of the potential litigation on March 12th of 2021, which was the same day that the Township reached out to the insurance company and also the day Delran filed an appeal of Judge Covert's decision to overturn the variance. Three days after Delran filed for the appeal, Dunphy's attorney's sent a letter to the court requesting that Solicitor Siciliano be sanctioned. The insurance company is of the position that the Township should have reached out to them back in September of 2020 when the Dunphy first filed his appeal, but instead of doing so, they were offering to buy Dunphy's property, so on April 9th of 2021, the insurance company denied the claim. The Township threatened arbitration on the matter and instead of fighting with the Town, the insurer gave $75,000 in what Council called a "kickback".

The Council approved the $300,000 taxpayer funded settlement at the May 4th of 2021 Council meeting, reading a statement into the record that was never posted online and with a written resolution that didn't include the amount of the settlement. It was not until Rabble Rouser Media began our investigation into the Township that the citizens of Delran ever learned about the settlement. It was hidden in what can only be called a cover up.

Just a month after the settlement was paid to the Dunphy's, a complaint was received by the Township from Bryan and Julie Weimer regarding Dunphy Landscaping. Even though the case had already been settled and a court already ruled on the case, Catrambone let them know that the Township was trying to find ways to enforce the laws against Dunphy. On June 8th of 2021, Mayor Catrambone and Council Person Lynn Jenney, paid a visit to the Weimer's to discuss how they can be of help regarding their issues with the Dunphy property. It seems though that the Weimers had already been helping Catrambone, because they sent several drone images of Dunphy's property in an April 19th of 2021 in an email that was sent to Catrambone. So not only was Catrambone playing detective at 4101 Bridgeboro Road, so were the Weimers.

On September 24th, 2021 a call was made to Delran police from Dunphy's landscaping regarding constant harassment from one of the neighbors. The neighbor is not named but their address is, which is none other than the address of the Weimers.

The settlement with the Dunphy's was negotiated by the Mayor and the Solicitor, both of whom were surely to be named as defendants in the potential litigation, the same litigation that would have also named the Zoning Board and its members, which included both Marlowe Smith and Lynn Jenney. All four interested parties should have recused themselves from the discussions and voting, yet they didn't. They instead avoided proper insurance filing requirements and used taxpayers dollars to cover their misdeeds and thought it would never see the light of day again. Sadly for them though, they had one hell of a party with fireworks that brought the Rabble Rouser to town who took the covers off of the crooks and exposed the corruption. Just another story, from where the sun don't shine!

Delran's Solicitor Resigns Amid Controversies. Duff Attacked.

Mayor Gary Catrambone released a video message letting the people of Delran know that Delran's Solicitor, Sal Siciliano, would not be resigning as the Council President had asked him to do, and would instead be providing a memo to explain some of the unanswered questions that have haunted the administration for months.

Those questions have been asked mainly by First Amendment activist and former Delran resident Patrick Duff, who has personally grilled the Council, Mayor, and the Solicitor over questions regarding the planning of the Lloyd Celebration, the inflated trash contracts, and most of all, the Township's treatment of Dunphy's Landscaping. The memo promised by the Mayor was never produced by Siciliano, who instead, shocked the Township and turned in his immediate resignation on February 21st.

During the last two Council meetings several comments have been made about Duff, including Council Person Tom Lyon calling him a "Carpetbagging, Self Serving, disingenuous person looking to make money from lawsuits." He went on to claim that Duff and "his lackey" were staring at him and making faces during the Council hearings. Lynn Jenney claimed that Duff and "his lackey" got within two inches of his face in an aggressive manner, causing him to need police escorts to and from the building.

Wendy Mitchell, Delran's Communications Director, claimed that because of Duff's inquiries, this is the first time Council, the Mayor and herself need police escorts to their cars. She went onto say that because of an image that Duff shared on his blog of her publicly available FaceBook page, which included a photo of Mitchell and Carli Lloyd and a background image of her son, that the "police department and Council have determined it was probably unsafe for me (her) to bring her 5 year old son to Winterfest", a claim that the police nor the Council could substantiate.

Back in October, just two weeks after Duff published his first story about the Carli Party, he received an online threat to shoot him in the face that warned him that he better stay offline, the threat also included several homosexual slurs and the person claimed to be a cop. Duff has also been the victim of a hit blog created that claims he faked having cancer to sell CBD products, he stole money from the MLK memorial in Maple Shade, and several other stores to try and defame the activist and deter him from his investigations. From the information gathered thus far, the author of the hit blog, and/or the person feeding them information, is most likely a very high ranking member of the Burlington County Democratic Committee, a fact that once confirmed the person's name will be released.

In November of 2021 a Delran resident named Michael Bigaj, decided to make a political hit video against Duff, where he used his own daughters as actors in the piece in an attempt to again defame the activist.

Just four days after Duff posted his first article, the Mayor posted a message that said a "nonresident" was making claims that "bribery and coercion" took place with regards to a donation to the Lloyd Party. This message was joined by a message on Carli Lloyd's fan page, where Lloyd herself attempted to silence the activist by using her platform of almost two million followers to tell "Patrick Duffy" to stop questioning things in Delran, which only seems to have made Duff dig deeper. The Mayor's Facebook page is controlled by Mitchell, who has been operating without any insurance for the entire year of 2021 up until January 17th of this year. When the Mayor was asked what Mitchell's qualifications for that position were, the Mayor stuttered and claimed that she was an entrepreneur and that he was training her, yet he did not state any valid qualifications as to why Mitchell was awarded the position.

It seems that Mitchell has been drafted to handle a new responsibility in town, the responsibility of hiring a new Solicitor. In a recent Burlington County Times posting it shows that all applications shall be delivered in a sealed envelope, attention to Delran's "Communications Director", which is Mitchell.

Duff recently filed a lawsuit against the Township for violating OPRA laws, a move the Township Council could have avoided by just filling the request. But instead the Township will be forced to pay tens of thousands of dollars in attorney fees to Duff's attorney CJ Griffin, as well as the temporary Solicitor to defend it if Duff wins. Council People Lynn Jenney and Tom Lyon claimed that Duff makes money from the OPRA suits that he and his attorney file, yet he has yet to see a dime from the many OPRA lawsuits he has been involved with, with Duff winning every one of the eight he has filed.

While OPRA lawsuits do not pay damages directly to the Plaintiff, defamation and retaliation suits do, which is something the Township might want to alert their insurance about this time, because that will be Duff's next move.

CHAPTER 9
"Senile Or A Liar"

After Sal's departure Delran hired the Wiener Law group as their new solicitor, who I coined the Dirty Wieners, as you will see why later. The Dirty Wieners were now not only defending Delran against the OPRA violation lawsuit that CJ Griffin filed on my behalf, but they were also representing Joseph Andl, who is not only the Executive Director of the Burlington County Bridge Commission, but he is also the chairman of the Burlington County Democratic Committee.

You see, in January, 2022 I sent an OPRA request to the Burlington County Bridge Commission seeking information regarding the suicide of a young man from Delran named Mason Williams, who tragically took his own life on January 7th of 2022 by jumping from the Tacony Palmyra Bridge. Mason's story touched me deeply, so I wrote a story about his life and passing that touched on some serious issues surrounding his suicide. Such as him wearing large signs that said "Suicide is more important than homecoming" just months prior to him jumping from the bridge.

Not long after posting the story, which included me questioning the way the school board handled the situation leading up to his suicide, Mason's mother made a rather cryptic post regarding a story that was being shared that she didn't agree with. While she didn't mention which story or who wrote it, it was obvious she was referring to my story. Even though I disagreed with what she was saying, which she was claiming the story was spreading misconceptions, I took the story down. All of the claims in the story were not coming from me, they were coming from people I interviewed who had a direct connection to Mason. May he rest in peace.

Those wanting to know more about Mason Williams and the foundation that his parents started for him can go to www.themasonwilliamsfoundation.org to learn more.

The powers that be saw this as the first real chink in my armor though, so they figured that they would use what they saw as my folly to prove just how big of a piece of shit I was. I had no idea that Andl worked at the Bridge when I sent the OPRA request regarding the suicide. But after seeing an internal version of the OPRA request that was copied and pasted on the hit blog about me in a story saying I was a sicko for wanting the information regarding the suicide, I knew someone at the Bridge was either working with the blogger, or the blogger themselves.

What I haven't told you yet is that Andl and I have had somewhat of a contentious relationship in the past due to him being the former Township Manager of Maple Shade, which is the town where Martin Luther King Jr's civil rights career began, which is a story that I have been researching for nearly a decade.

I know what some of you are thinking, what does Maple Shade and Martin Luther King Jr's civil rights career have in common? Well, it was the site of the first sit-in that King had ever participated in, as well as where King first testified in court in a civil rights case after he and three friends were not only denied service at a cafe, but they were also chased out by the owner, Ernest Nichols, who was shooting a pistol into the air yelling "I've killed for less".

As I mentioned earlier, that book is still stuck in edit, but if you Google my name and MLK you will find dozens of articles relating to my work there, which included a plaque that I "worked" with Andl on having placed in Maple Shade. I say "worked"because Andl did everything to work against me, even having me raise money for the plaque only to claim the town cannot accept it, and then putting the plaque up without ever telling me.

One of the other stories on the hit blog claimed that I stole that same money that Andl had me raise for the plaque, money that Andl told me I could give directly to the vendor once the order was complete, only to never contact me so I could provide it to the vendor. I only learned about the plaque being erected after confronting a whack job named Vincent Squire, who was part of a radio program put on by a Republican candidate for Congress named Paul Dilks, that for some odd reason, was dedicated to shaming me and my MLK project.

While confronting Squire in a gas station parking lot where he and Dilks were taping, he let me know that he had just returned from Maple Shade where the town manager told him that the plaque that I had raised the money for, had already been installed by Andl. Squire blew up as if the plaque already being installed was proof that I stole the funds, the same story that just happened to appear on the same blog with the OPRA request from the Bridge Commission.

Armed with this information I filed a defamation lawsuit against Joseph Andl and John Doe, because I had a hunch that Andl wasn't the only one involved in the blog. My hunch was that it was someone from within the Delran Mayor's troll army who wrote the blog, and most likely, Queen Trollzilla herself, Wendy Mitchell. But I couldn't yet prove it. You see, Mitchell, Catrambone and Andl all sit on the Burlington County Democratic Committee, so they run protection for each other.

With Mitchell claiming that she couldn't attend the Winterfest with her child due to my inquiries, and Lying Lynn Jeney claiming that he needed a police escort due to me, I knew they were desperate to get me in some type of trouble. The then recently released video of the incident clearly showed that neither myself, nor my claimed "lackey" Scott Ducko, ever got two inches from Jeney's face, screaming at him, as he alleged. The police also denied Jeney and Mitchell's claims of the need for them to get escorts to and from the meetings. So I knew that I had to be careful at the next meeting so as to not give them any chance to cry foul again, as you'll read below.

Minutes From March 8th, 2022 Council Meeting.

Ms. Littleton stated that she believes Mr. Siciliano provided advice to the Township that they did not need to notify the JIF with regards to Dunphy's appeal. If that is the case, has anyone from the Township looked into the possibility of filing a claim against his insurance.

Mr. Catrambone stated that he does not know if that has been stated. This was handled by the prior Administrator and he does not believe it resulted in the Township not being covered for the claim. He is not sure what claim we would have against the insurance company.

Ms. Littleton said that what the Township endured was paying out $300,000 minus the $75,000 that the insurance covered based upon the advice that you didn't need to contact the JIF.

Mr. Catrambone stated that he does not believe that we received that advice. Mr. Catrambone stated that is something we can look into.

Ms. Littleton stated that she did submit an OPRA for a cost summary for CME Associates site survey of the Dunphy's property. She asked what the purpose of the site survey was.

Mr. Burrell stated that the purpose of the survey was that the

Township had an interest in purchasing the property. There was discussion on the wetland boundaries on the property.

Ms. Littleton asked if the Township had access to the property for the survey.

Mr. Catrambone stated yes, we received Dunphy's approval to access the property. Ms. Littleton asked if the Township has a business license for WL Mitchell. Mr. Catrambone stated that we have all the licenses needed for a consultant.

Ms. Littleton stated that as part of an OPRA request, some documents have been provided and there was a business registration for Wendy Mitchell but not WL Mitchell. Ms. Littleton stated that she is not sure if that could cause an issue with the insurance.

Mr. Burrell stated that the CFO has verified that she has all the required documents.

Mr. Catrambone stated that they will look at this issue again.

Patrick Duff, Haddon Heights resident, stated that he waited outside because there have been comments from Mr. Jeney that someone from his posse got within two inches of his face and that is an absolute lie. Mr. Duff asked Mr. Jeney when this happened.

Mr. Jeney stated that he believes it was the first time he spoke at the meeting. Mr. Jeney stated that he was walking out the front door along with Mr. Lyon and as they went out the door he asked that everyone in the lobby put their masks on, which was required at the time, and Mr. Dusko jumped in his face and starting screaming that Mr. Burrell did not have his mask on before the meeting and he continued as they walked out and following them down the sidewalk. Mr. Duff then called Mr. Dusko back. Mr. Jeney asked if Mr. Duff remembers that event.

Mr. Duff stated that he does not.

Mr. Jeney stated that Mr. Duff is a liar.

Mr. Duff stated that Mr. Jeney is either senile or a liar.

Mr. Jeney stated that there were other people there at that time.

Mr. Duff stated that he purposely didn't come in until after the meeting started so he could not lie again and will leave right after.

Mr. Duff asked why Mr. Jeney didn't press charges.

Mr. Jeney stated that he was the bigger man and walked away.

Mr. Duff stated that he has been coming here for five months and Mr. Jeney waited until last week to tell that this happened. This only happened after he came on the hot seat because he should have recused himself on Dunphy's litigation. Mr. Duff stated that he received bad advice from the Township Attorney. Mr. Duff stated that he never claimed to receive $7,000 from any municipality. He did tell them that he would sue the Township and win, which will happen, as he believes the Township will settle tonight and if they don't that would be silly. There was no reason to redact the faces. He wanted to show that the event was not well attended.

Mr. Jeney stated that he will rely on anyone that was there if they want to be honest, they can testify that is exactly what happened. He is not in the habit of lying. Mr. Jeney stated that Mr. Duff is talking about so many false facts and then he weaves them into a narrative. Mr. Jeney stated that he has nothing else to say.

Mr. Duff stated that he is done coming to Delran. When someone makes a false allegation that someone threatened them, it is also the point that someone will make up lies. Mr. Duff stated that if they received bad advice from the Solicitor, that is one thing but just admit it. Mr. Duff stated that Mr. Jeney should have recused himself from the Dunphy litigation. Mr. Duff stated that the

Township did not go through the insurance company and did not file on time. Mr. Duff stated that he is asking Mayor and Mr. Jeney for an apology and/or the Township faces a defamation suit. There is a blog about him out there saying that he faked his cancer. The Mayor and Council are legitimizing that with their attitude.

Mr. Jeney stated that is not true, this is the tale he weaves.

Mr. Duff stated that the only people to mention the blog were the Mayor and Mr. Burrell at a Council meeting. Mr. Duff stated that he will catch the individual responsible for the blog.

Minutes From March 22nd, 2022 Delran Council Meeting.

Mr. Burrell reported that Delran Township has come to a settlement agreement with Patrick Duff. He explained that this highlights the importance of having a Township Solicitor that has good knowledge of OPRA requests because these matters do impact us financially.

Mr. Egan referenced video footage regarding an encounter Mr. Jeney had with Mr. Duff and Mr. Dusko. Based on that footage, he asked if Mr. Jeney would like to apologize for accusing them of getting within two inches of his face since the video did not show that.

Mr. Jeney stated that he will not offer an apology since the video failed to capture the full encounter in the doorway once everyone left the building.

Ms. Littleton commented on the video footage and stated that the only time that Mr. Dusko came close to Mr. Jeney's face was when they were walking through the door.

Mr. Jeney responded that Mr. Dusko approached him with a loud voice and startled him and then continued to follow him down the walkway mocking him.

Ms. Littleton questioned why the video of the Carli Lloyd Event wasn't released right away.

Mr. Catrambone explained that due to the environment that was created, he was being very cautious about everything. Ms. Littleton stated that it gives the perception that something else was going on.

Transcript of PUBLIC MEETING
AUGUST 9, 2022

Patrick Duff: So, real quick, Congratulations. BTW I don't know if anybody saw my predictions earlier online. I predicted every candidate you picked, and I predicted that you would be sitting there (pointing at the new Council person who replaced another one with no mouth). I call myself the swami of salami. political predictions by Patrick Fuff. uh go back and look right on the Facebook page Delran resident's official page, the page that your Communications Director never posts on.

Mayor Catrambone: Would you like to know why that is? Because they uh prior to her becoming Communications Director didn't agree with what she was posting and they haven't let her on that page. She would post on that if she could.

Patrick Duff: You maybe should find somebody to try to post on the page. That's 8,500 people on that page. and it's funny because a couple weeks ago somebody called me and said hey, "we're having issues with the ambulances. There's no ambulances working in town" so I called the ambulance service and I got some confirmation of that, and I wrote an article and I put it out. My article said nothing bad, it didn't create any emergency in anybody's mind, literally just pointed out the facts. Then a statement comes out from the Township to watch out for communications coming from other sources. That's ridiculous, I mean nothing I said in my article was bad. Let me ask you if there is a protocol, because we're talking about these emails, these phishing emails that come in. Is there a protocol where you don't open attachments to emails if they're sent from an unknown source?

Mayor Catrambone: We have extensive training. That only emails...

Patrick Duff: That you don't you don't click a link from an unknown source?

Mayor Catrambone: Yeah.

Patrick Duff: So how did you click the link that came in from the blog? How did you find out about the blog that was written about me that said I faked my cancer? That came in from the blogger, the sunlight disinfects 2022. How did you know about it? You had to have clicked on the link.

Mayor Catrambone: It was sent a year ago. I don't remember how I found out about it. It came to me anonymously.

Patrick Duff: No, it came to you in an email from an unknown source. Did you open the link?

Mayor Catrambone: It's hard to remember a year ago, because, but, I'm sure I saw it, because...

Patrick Duff: Well you had to, because you commented on what was on the blog.

Mayor Catrambone: I may have, I may have copied the link and uh… typed it in directly. So it wouldn't be..

Patrick Duff: Your memory is getting better now, huh?

Mayor Catrambone: Uh, yeah.

Patrick Duff: No. You clicked on the link because you knew who it came from, because it came from inside the source of Delran. I've got a mole here letting me know that.

Mayor Catrambone: Really?

Patrick Duff: Yup, Yup.

Mayor Catrambone: Care to share who that is?

Patrick Duff: Care to share who the "non-resident" is?

Mayor Catrambone: Which non-resident

Patrick Duff: Exactly, you see I love this, the political sparring that I have with Delran just makes me so much better for the other towns, and you (pointing at Mayor) are the biggest beaute I have ever met in politics, because you literally will create new stories on top of other stories. Do you realize that a lie on top of a lie just makes it more difficult to remember what you're saying? I mean that is probably your worst political, uh political move, is that you continue to lie. The blog came to you through an outside party third email and you opened it, isn't that right?

Solicitor: The Council members and the Mayor are not here to answer every question and frankly we know you have a lawsuit about some blog and your issues.

Patrick Duff: Correct.

Solicitor: I don't see why we should be having this discussion.

Patrick Duff: Because it came from this, mam. It came from my experiences in Delran, and somebody is telling me that it came from the inside of Delran. How about an investigation, would you launch an investigation?

Solicitor: Sir we are not going to do any investigation at this point because of what you say. You have a lawsuit about the blog.

Patrick Duff: And I have yet to name anybody in the lawsuit here in Delran.

Solicitor: But you stated that, and then in this room, you point to several people, and then you want to come up here and talk about this. It's not appropriate.

Patrick Duff: Sure it's appropriate.

Solicitor: I'm not so sure that anyone here is interested in your personal business.

Patrick Duff: You know what's interesting about that? This is free speech, this is my opportunity to speak.

Solicitor: Right.

Patrick Duff: So with my opportunity to speak, not only have I exposed that there was a $300,000 settlement that was covered up by the town, that there was a trash contract that 45% higher than the previous contract that was only one bid, that there was bid splitting and all of these other things I've uncovered. So what I have come up here and said actually has made a difference, ok? There should be an investigation because there is somebody in town that helped write the blog that claimed I faked cancer to steal money from people. If you think that's right, you're crazy.

CHAPTER 10
Blogger Busted & Bids Were Split.

Even though the entire administration denied bid splitting occurred, Delran's own audit came back and found that they did in fact illegally split the bids to throw the biggest retirement party ever. I met Tyler Burrell for a drink and a conversation after the bid splitting was confirmed, where Tyler told me that the Auditor said that not only should have the video screens and stage been included into one contract, but all of the other services, such as porta potties and fireworks, should have been included into one also so they all could be bid on together.

The day after the August 9th meeting I got a call from a person who not only worked for the Township, but was also well connected to the Democratic County Committee. They told me that they knew first hand that Wendy Mitchell was telling people that I had faked my very real cancer. They also let me know that the last two digits of Mitchell's phone number just happened to match the last two digits of the Gmail account that had created the vile blog about me.

Resetting a password on a Gmail account can be done in several different ways, with the most common being users inputting their cell phone number to do so. If you get one digit wrong, it will not send the reset message and ask for confirmation. But if you enter the number correctly, you get a message asking you to input the reset code that was texted to the corresponding phone number.

When I entered Mitchell's phone number that she had listed on Delran's website for herself as the Communications Director, it asked for the verification code, proving that Mitchell was the author of the blog, and probably causing Mitchell to shit herself.

After sending proof to the Township of my findings, Mitchell was immediately terminated. But she didn't go quietly. No. She wrote a strange and almost threatening message on FaceBook, saying she'll "be waiting in the tall grass.". Whatever the fuck that means?

Now that I had clear proof of who wrote the blog, I reached out to an attorney who specializes in defamation of character cases, Corinne Mullen, who I retained right away. I also contacted the local press to let them know about the wild situation that was going on, and Carol Comengo of the Courier Post reached out and agreed to do a story. Comengo and I were set to meet at the next Council meeting on August 23rd, which as you will see, was quite a wild public meeting.

Delran Officials Fire Town's Communications Director After Patrick Duff Proves She Is The Blogger Who Claimed He Faked Cancer. 8-11-22

Delran Township has been at the center of a great deal of controversy over the last several months, which is all due to the exposure created by a local advocate for government transparency, Patrick Duff, who began his inquiries into the town last October. Since that time Duff has uncovered several unethical, immoral, and even illegal acts that were committed by Township officials, mostly pointing directly to Delran's Mayor, Gary Catrambone. Last year Catrambone created the position of Communications Director, and filled the position with a person who lacked any real credentials for the job, Wendy

Mitchell.

Mitchell was terminated yesterday by Delran Officials after Duff outed her as the owner of a blog that was written in January of this year that claimed Duff faked having cancer to steal money from other cancer patients, and unsuspecting others. The blog also contained a story about how Duff stole money that he raised for a memorial in Maple Shade dedicated to Martin Luther King Jr and his first civil rights battle.

Last July Duff was diagnosed with colon cancer after a colonoscopy found a massive tumor that had been misdiagnosed for several years as diverticulitis. Just a week after being diagnosed, Duff underwent a ten and a half hour surgery where they removed a perforated cancerous tumor that measured nearly ten inches, which meant the tumor was leaking cancer into his body. Miraculously the cancer did not spread to the Lymph-nodes or any other organ, yet the chances of the cancer returning were high, and Duff was diagnosed as a high risk stage two cancer patient.

Duff recently filed suit against the Executive Director of the Burlington County Bridge Commission, who is also the Chairman of the Burlington County Democratic Committee, Joe Andl, for feeding documents and information that appeared on the once anonymous blogger's website, who was named as a John Doe in the suit. Now that the identity of the owner of the blog has been identified, the John Doe name in the suit will now be replaced by the name of Wendy Mitchell, as well as adding Delran Township as a defendant in a recently filed defamation lawsuit. (Case # CAM L-1716-22)

While Mitchell was listed as a Communications Director for Delran, her responsibilities and activities showed that she was much more of a private assistant for Delran's Mayor, Gary Catrambone, who has been the target of the investigations by Duff into corruption involving Delran's government.

Catrambone released a statement on January 4th of this year where he said "I have personally requested an audit by the State Comptroller and a review by the State Ethics Board."This was a statement that was only compelled by Duff's investigations into the Township.

The day after the Mayor called for his own investigation the political hit blog was created against Duff, with the very first story claiming he stole money from a memorial that Duff lobbied the township of Maple Shade to install that was dedicated to Martin Luther King, and two days later the blog posted a story that claimed Duff was faking his very real cancer to steal money from other cancer patients.

Months have gone by since the blog was published, with Duff thinking nonstop about how to bring the blogger to justice, which happened yesterday after Duff devised a plan that would prove the blogger's identity. It was only hours after Duff figured out how to identify the blogger ,and shared it with Delran officials, that Mitchell was terminated. Mitchell, who claims to have consulted an attorney, released her own very odd, and very long, statement regarding her getting fired, where she claimed that someone set her up, and also makes strange comments about "waiting in the tall grass".

Council President Tyler Burrell released a short statement yesterday that simply said "Please be advised that WLMitchell Consulting is no longer Delran Township's Communicator Director. In the interim, all communication will be handled by the Administrator and his office.", yet nothing has been said since.

We now await an official statement from the Township of Delran regarding the extremely controversial situation, which will just be one more chapter in what has been dubbed, The Delran Debacle. (Netflix series, soon to come.)

WORK SESSION Transcript August 23rd 2022 MUNICIPAL BUILDING DELRAN, NJ

Joe Joyce: Good evening. Joseph Joyce, I live in Delran, New Jersey. I will not be giving my street address out. I will get into reasons why I'm not giving my street address out. Over the past year people who have spoken out at this podium have received death threats, in their social media inboxes, and have had their tires slashed. That was brought to Council's attention by the way by a man named Tony Egan. I went back and watched that meeting.

This has gone on long enough, and with the termination of the contract with the Communications Director last week over allegations that are too disgusting to even say. I mean, who does that? Who would say that someone faked cancer? The cancer was covered in Newsweek, there are pictures of a tumor that is this big (holding hands apart 10 or so inches). How can someone say that that was fake, and hold a public position? This happened back in January, and it is now August and she held that position until now. As someone who has lost relatives to cancer, that was disgusting to read. It was hurtful to read. I can only imagine what the person who was about, felt like.

This has gone on long enough. I congratulated each one of you in 2020, when you won. I think I lost more than anyone. I believe Tyler, you beat me three to one. Mr Jeney, I believe you were two and a half to one, congratulations again. By the way, I have the utmost respect for each one of your offices and each one of you, however I am disgusted by the actions that have taken place over the past year. I do not speak for any other resident other than myself, and I hope that other residents speak up, but people are afraid to in Delran because of retaliation.

There's one common thread among all the people who have received threats, had issues in the schools with their kids, and it's they've spoken up at this podium about the issues that have occurred, and that has to stop! And the ultimate act of retaliation, was what happened to Mr. Duff, where a blog was written about him. Then when he showed the evidence, it was denied and when I read that post (by Mitchell) on the resident's official page "waiting in the tall grass". That can be interpreted as a threat!

This has to stop. Mr Catrambone, I have the utmost respect for the office of the mayor. I congratulated you. I talked to Wendy months ago about having a job fair in Delran, about being productive. Being an active member of my community regardless of party, regardless of politics, and in return we have this to deal with. Mr. Catrambone, you won the election fair and square. You won the election. You beat Pat Pomeranz. You are the Mayor. However, the actions over the past year have proven that you do not care about the residents of this town, you care about yourself. And I respectfully ask you to resign your position as Mayor. I ask you to resign.

I am asking as a citizen of Delran, as a resident who cares about his community, and as someone who has heard enough horror stories from people who have received death threats. Someone threatened to shoot that man in the face. He received a message. Other people, like Mark Oberg, received threats in his inbox. People had their tires slashed over this, and I'm not saying that anyone on Council or you, or anyone here directed that, but that's the climate that we have in this town, and it needs to stop.

Mr. Catrambone you care about Delran, I believe that's why you got into politics. I'm asking you please, as a citizen, as someone who at one time thought that you were a pretty good Councilman years ago, please resign. This is not a political statement, this is a citizen coming to Council, and to the Mayor

145

and asking for a resignation over absolutely horrible decisions. I yield the rest of my time. (Loud applause from packed house)

Councilman Burrell: Thank you very much. I appreciate that. I will say I'm not going to comment on everything because we'll be here all night. I do have to say, you know, it is unacceptable that there's retaliation of any kind going on. No matter what your political party is. So none of us stand for that, I can assure you of that. If there are those types of problems, please please please, this is not the medium to bring it up in though. We are not the reporting agency. So please contact the police. You know they are an apolitical body, they will investigate and do the job that they need to do. So if that does happen please continue to report to the police. Is there any other public comments please raise your hand slowly

Barbara Littleton: Barb littleton, I reside here in Delran, again I do not want to state my address. I've had people come up to my door, so I really don't want to say my address.

I want to reiterate the comments that were just made. Over the past year we've had numerous issues with what's going on here, the decisions that are being made, and all of them have the same one person that is pretty much the crux of it all. Mayor, I think you're a good person at heart. I just think that some of the decisions you made are personal in nature for you, and not in the best interest of this township.

When you took on the Dunphy case, and a couple other people on the Council who had some responsibility with that case as well, we settled out of court for three hundred thousand dollars. If you look at the net, no matter what it's three hundred thousand dollars to the taxpayers when the insurance company could have covered that. So whether you did it personally, or the business administrator did it before, or whatever happened.

Whatever reason that didn't get reported to the insurance company, it comes back to you! It comes back to the Council, because you have an obligation to uphold the internal controls to make sure this township works the way it's supposed to. So, with that we're looking at that, we're looking at the Carli Lloyd event, and the debacle with that, and and all the different things that we identified with that.

Now we get this Communications Director position, which we have been hounding the Council, and you Mayor, over for the last year. We've been asking questions: what's happening? Are we covered as residents if this person does something and a court case comes out. Are we covered? Well come to find out we're not. Her insurance was not valid at the point of the post. So, I mean, we can all look at that. Mayor, I know you were crux in getting that position filled, and hiring that person. You had her for a year in a temporary position, and then this year the Council went ahead and hired her again.

The due diligence that you got just wasn't there, or at least what you provided to us was not there. With all of these decisions, I agree. I would ask you for your resignation. Thank you so much [Applause]

Councilman Burrell: If there are any other comments, please raise your hand. Mr. Duff.

Patrick Duff: All right, how are you doing ? You know, the last time two weeks ago I came here and I asked your associate to start an investigation, because I had some people that were telling me that the person that created the blog was actually Wendy Mitchell and that she was going around this municipal building telling people that she saw my medical records, and that it proved that I didn't have cancer.

Now I didn't have a c-section, but I have a scar from the top of my pelvis to near the middle of my chest. I had a 10 inch tumor removed from my body about a year ago. One of the most difficult things you'll ever hear in your life, if you get to hear this, are the words "you have cancer". It feels like the world hit a pause button and left you behind. You feel like you're given a death sentence. You're just 45 years old, an 11 year old son sitting at home, and I thought I was going to die.

That's why I did this crap, because I was sitting in a hospital saying, well pardon my French but this "effing" world is so bad right now. There's no honesty. There's no adults in the room. There's no transparency in government. I mean people are stealing from the poor, and people are people just doing nothing about it. So I decided I wanted to do something about it, and I did.

What's so funny though is I didn't even look at the whole Carli Lloyd thing seriously. I was just gonna just use my skills to show how much his party cost. But you hid the cost of the party. Like the whole way it's been a hidden agenda, everything in the dark, and people who operate in the shadows do the stuff like happen to me. They create a blog that says I faked cancer. There's a woman in Delran who did fake cancer, and I think she got like five years probation. A man in California just got seven years in prison for faking cancer and stealing money. Five years in New York, I mean I look at this every day.

My wife went to Thailand two months ago. When she left for Thailand I paid for a vacation and I said, I'm going to be there, I'm going to come. I'll see you in a couple weeks. I said I'm staying home so I can write my book about Martin Luther King. That was a lie! I lied to my wife. (getting emotional) I stayed home so I could find that person who wrote that fucking blog about me. Pardon my french. (applause) And nobody understands that. I couldn't sleep. I couldn't breathe when she left thinking about that. Think about that. Somebody goes searching the internet and they find that. What do they think about you at that point?

Mayor, did you agree with that blog post? Do you agree with what it says? Do you think it was valuable in any way? Do you support the author of it?

Mayor Catrambone: So we have, I stated immediately when that blog came out, that I denounced that blog and didn't agree with what it was. And it wasn't Delran, and there was nothing that I did ever to promote anything about that blog.

Duff: Your personal assistant wrote the blog.

Mayor Catrambone: I don't believe she did so.

Duff: So you don't believe she did? Do you think she was set up? Come on, tell the people.

Catrambone: I don't know. I don't believe she wrote it

Duff: So her phone number is attached to the blog. Her cell phone is directly attached to the blog. Do you understand how that works technology wise?

Catrambone: I have a pretty good grasp of technology, yeah.

Duff: So why did she get fired immediately , Mayor?

Catrambone: I didn't have anything to do with that.

Duff: No? Mayor, you were at her house three days after that she was fired weren't you, hanging out? You were at a birthday party.

Catrambone: Oh yeah, we were.

Duff: Yeah you were. So you basically condoned her act.

Catrambone: Is that what that is?

Duff: That's what it is to me.

Catrambone: It's a child's birthday party.

Duff: You're attending a child's birthday party with somebody that was literally just sent a letter saying she wasn't even allowed back in the municipal building, and you're now saying how she was set up, so tell us how she was set up?

Catrambone: I didn't say she was set up. I don't know what happened.

Duff: Mayor on January 4th you released a statement this year to call for an investigation yourself. Nobody has heard anything about the investigation yet, you haven't said anything. You said you're going to release a letter that was going to explain the timeline of the Dunphy scandal. Never did that. You said you were going to release the investigation you called for, and the results, and you never did that. Now you are saying that she didn't write this blog. Mayor on January 4th you released the statement calling for your own investigation, and on January 5th the blog was created. Is that a coincidence? Do you think that's a coincidence? I don't. Just so you know, you said that I;m doing this for money or something? I'm surely not doing it for money. I haven't made a dollar off of all of these OPRA cases I have done. But I am going to, sue, man...Your Communications Director wrote a blog saying I faked cancer and that I stole money from a memorial. Do you know how liable you are at this point? I have the best defamation lawyer in NJ right now that I just signed a retainer with. (Loud applause)

Burrell: Mr Duff your time is up.

Duff: What is so crazy to me is that the second person that I named in the lawsuit, is the chair of the Burlington County Democratic party, hired you as an attorney too. (pointing to the dirty Weiner Solicitor) So how can the attorney for Delran Township, be the attorney for the other party, because you are going to be named also? See ya. (Applause)

Burrell from the minutes: Mr. Burrell thanked everyone who spoke or supported the speakers tonight by being at the meeting. He remarked that he shares the frustrations of the people who came to the meeting. All of the employees of the Township have had to deal with the current controversies. He stated that he feels the people want accountability. He explained that the Council has done their best to be accountable by previously getting rid of the Township Solicitor and by terminating the contract of the Communications Director this evening. Mr. Burrell stated that he would like answers from the mayor because until that happens, it will be very difficult to get anything except the day to day running of the Township done. He discussed the standard of conduct that is acceptable for elected officials. He advised that the Mayor should strongly consider what the residents have suggested tonight.

Mr. Catrambone: Stated that he appreciated the comments of Mr. Burrell but he noted that everything related to Dunphy's was Council approved. The Carli Lloyd Event was handled by Council and the RAC. Mr. Catrambone explained that this is a heartbreaking situation but that he was elected to do a job and he has no intention of resigning.

Audit Finds Delran Officials Illegally Split Bids In The Planning Of Carli Lloyd Party. 9-26-2022

The recently released 2021 audit of Delran Township's finances shows that township officials were not in compliance with N.J.S.A 40A: 11-7(Contracts not to be divided), when the Township "paid $61,500 to two vendors that were related to a Township celebratory event held in October 2021". The audit states that "The Township paid two vendors for the performance of services that in the aggregate exceeded the bid threshold.".

The planning of the Carli Lloyd retirement party will now cost the taxpayers even more money as Delran needs to hire three new lawyers to represent those Officials involved in the planning of the "biggest (retirement) party ever".

The Agenda for tomorrow night's council meeting includes "Resolution 2022-174 Approving the Corrective Action Plan Based on the Recommendations in the 2021 Audit Report", with three separate resolutions to hire "special counsel" for three unnamed Delran officials.

The "cause" stated in the audit claims "The Township officials, including the Recreation Advisory Committee, were under the advice that these were two separate contracts for different services and were not subject to bid. However, Local Public Contract Law states that goods or services in connection with the same immediate purpose or task should be considered together. If these contracts were aggregated, they would have exceeded the bid threshold and therefore, could have been bid, depending on the timing of providing the service.".

That advice came from Delran's former Solicitor Sal Siciliano, who resigned earlier this year after Council President Tyler Burrell publicly demanded his resignation due to Siciliano's poor legal advice on several controversial issues. In that same meeting, Council President Burrell expressed his frustration with Mayor Gary Catrambone, saying that he would ask Catrambone to resign, but the Mayor wouldn't listen anyway.

Council President Burrell minced no words though at last month's Council meeting, where he directly asked for the Mayor's resignation in a long and emotional statement that was read into the record, asking for "accountability" from the Mayor. The request for the Mayor's resignation last month was due to a blog that was created by Delran's former Communications Director, Wendy Mitchell, who was the right hand gal to the Mayor. Mitchell created a blog about activist, and CEO of Rabble Rouser Media, Patrick Duff, claiming Duff faked his very real cancer to profit by ripping off unsuspecting cancer patients.

The Mayor not only refused to resign, but he also refused to even acknowledge Mitchell's obvious involvement, claiming that he didn't believe Mitchell was involved, and insinuated that she was set up in some type of way.

The Mayor strongly claimed that nothing illegal or unethical was done during the planning of the Carli Lloyd event. But now that the Township's own auditors have confirmed that illegal activity did take place, what will the Mayor's new claim be?

CHAPTER 11

Post Delran Debacle Breakdown

A couple of weeks after I began my siege on Delran politics, I contacted the Burlington County Prosecutor's Office to see if they'd be interested in the illegal activity that I had found. When the woman answered the phone and asked me what she could help me with, I told her that I am a local investigative journalist working on a story about corruption. The woman quickly asked, "Is this Patrick Duff?", which kind of shocked me, but I said yes. She went on to say that people in the office were watching my work like a little soap opera, and I even had a little cheering squad.

As soon as she said that I had a little cheering squad, I knew my plan was working. But I also knew I most likely was making some enemies. A friend of mine showed an image of a message that included my name on it to a receptionist at the Burlington Prosecutor's Office, and the woman working at the counter called me a "FaceBook Troublemaker"! Which felt just as good as knowing I had a little cheering squad.

A lot has changed in Delran due to my work, but a lot has also stayed the same. Wendy Mitchell was fired, Solicitor Sal resigned, the Mayor was asked to resign, and Tyler Burrell no longer sits on the town's Democratic Committee. Even though the one Republican candidate for Council lost, he came much closer than any Republican that has run in the last decade. But for now they'll just have more cover ups and back door deals handled in executive sessions and in Lynn Jeney's basement.

The Burlington County Prosecutor and the FBI investigated the activity in Delran, with the FBI even sitting down with Colin "The Kid" Rafferty for an interview about the bid splitting and self-dealing, but no charges were ever filed. The Burlngton County Prosecutor told me that while they did beak the law, it didn't reach their threshold to prosecute.

Carol Comnego of the Courier Post was at that explosive last meeting that you just read about. She even interviewed the Mayor, Burrell, several residents, and myself for an article she was writing on the debacle. Over the next couple of days we communicated regularly, with Comengo continually making more inquiries about the situation, and with me providing the answers. The story was set to be one of the biggest political scandals in Burlington County history, with hit blogs claiming people faked cancer, multiple calls for the Mayor's resignation by both residents and council members, and lawsuits against powerful people. It had everything.

Comengo and I went back and forth for several days until I started to wonder if she was ever going to go to print with the titillating tale of town's transgressions. Her tone began to change, and after a couple of days she just went silent, and the Courier Post officially killed the story. This ended any hope that I had for the mainstream media to cover the lawsuit, and it just solidified the need for an independent source of media to become more prominent in the local news cycle in the South Jersey area.

Thank God for Tyler Burrell stepping up for Delran and holding the Mayor to account though, right, or was that assumption wrong? Let's be honest here, the Delran Mayor had become toxic, so not only was it a politically savvy way for Burrell to distance himself from Catrambone, but it was also his way to make a hedge for control. Something that Tyler previously watched, and also helped Catrambone do to the former Mayor

Ken Paris.

Sadly it seems the party planning DJ's didn't learn from the exposure from the Delran Debacle though, because in the planning of the 2022 and 2023 Delran Night Out events, they also broke local public contract laws by not putting the events out for public bidding. The 2022 event cost around $55,000, and 2023 over $65,000, for just two small concerts with a cover band, fireworks and some bouncy houses. So with just three events, including the Carli Party, Delran put out more than $200,000, most of it being spent just on stages, and more than likely, greasing palms.

When I juxtaposed those costs with other municipalities close to Delran, it really looked bad. Cinnaminson, for example, will hold 11 concerts for 2023, including a nine concert summer series, a Juneteenth concert, and a concert for the Fall Festival. The total costs for all 11 concerts is just above $24,000, while Delran spent over $200,000 on just three concerts over the span of three years. I guess that's what you get when you let DJ's plan the party with other people's money. It also earned Tyler Burrell his new nickname, Big Spender Burrell.

The lawyer I hired to take over my case against Joe Andl and file an amended complaint against Delran Township, Corinne Mullen, wound up absolutely fucking me. Instead of her filing the amended complaint against Delran, she dismissed my entire case against Joe Andl with prejudice, meaning I can never file against his grimy ass again for defamation regarding the hit blog.

I wasn't going to let the other defendants get away with it though, so I refiled the lawsuit myself in another court against Delran Township, Wendy Mitchell, Mayor Gary Cat, and Lying Lynn Jeney, who both could have avoided being named if they just apologized when I gave them the chance to. While I cannot discuss the details of the settlement, I can say that there is a public resolution that has some of the details of the deal between the Township and myself. I can also say that the Mayor and Council tried to pull another fast one on the citizens though concerning the resolution for my settlement, because they approved it without the resolution being listed on the agenda. And even though one Council member voted no, and another abstained, the resolution that was made available to the public has all five members of council voting "yes" on approving the settlement.

By some unknown miracle, because Mitchell wouldn't ever admit to ownership of the blog, the hit blog mysteriously disappeared the day we settled.

A source let me know that after the Township unlawfully denied Dunphy's variance, rendering his property all but useless, the Township offered the Landscaping company double of what Dunphy had paid.

Delran officials never did go to the insurer on time, nor provide the insurance timeline that was promised. The Mayor and Sal, who were the main culprits in the alleged crimes against Dunphy, were the ones to negotiate the settlement that cleared them of the wrong doing. They used the houses own money to pay off those they personally wronged. Talk about a conflict?

I recently filed a legal malpractice lawsuit against Corinne Mullen and her law firm for fucking me on the Andl case. After she screwed me over I researched her a bit more and found out that at around the same time she took my case, she was also representing a high powered Democratic player, NJ Senator Ray Lesniak, in his own defamation case. Knowing that, my guess is that with Andl's position of power in the party, he somehow got someone to convince Mullen to screw me over. Because I can't think of any other reason why a lawyer would do that to their client. But no matter how you cut the cake, Corinne worked with a Dirty Weiner to fuck me.

BTW. Corinne Mullen, go fuck yourself! And I hope you lose your law license.

CHAPTER 12

The Bat Signal Above Medford

One party control at the local level gives more of an opportunity for nepotism, corruption, and fraud, as we just saw in Delran, who were all Democrats. Some in the political world were spreading rumors that I was being paid by the local GOP to take out the all Democratic Delran Council, but that just wasn't true. I am not affiliated with any one party, but I knew that if I just said I wasn't working for the GOP, I'd look like just another political hack. But I had a big problem. Where does one find any Republicans in South Jersey that control anything?

In May of 2022 I was contacted by one of my sources who let me know about a family in Medford that was being harassed by some local politicians and government officials. When he first told me, I was kind of disinterested, but after looking into what was happening, and also the fact that Medford was the only Republican stronghold in Burlington County, I accepted the mission.

I went to Medford to meet the Carns brothers and hear their story, and after talking to them for a while I thought that I could tell their tale in just three articles. But what I thought would be just three articles, has turned into more than a dozen, as well as a good friendship with Brian Carns that includes a trip where he joined me in Northern California to film a documentary I am making about a friend of mine who was murdered, so he's good people.

After looking over the materials that the Carns brothers gave to me, the pattern of harassment and retaliation was clear. The Pine Barrens Tribune had already written about the situation, but I felt like the article was a bit too long for people's short attention spans today, and I also felt like this was going to take more than just writing, this was going to take some real deal public Rabble Rousing and salesmanship to get more eyes on the story. Knowing that sex sells, and the beef was over firewood that Mayor Chuck Watson didn't pay for, I named my first article "Stiffed Wood". And the Mayhem in Medford was born.

Stiffed Wood. Part 1 of
The Mayhem In Medford. 5-13-22

The Carns Family tree farm has been in existence for more than 80 years, located in the sparse suburban community of Medford, New Jersey, a medium-sized township with just under 25,000 residents. The 80 year old Matriarch of the family, Carolyn Carns, has spent her entire life on the farm, where she raised her five children who help operate a tree service company that their late father founded in the 1960's. Carolyn, who now must use a wheelchair to get around her property, was recently threatened with massive fines and jail time for parking more than one commercial vehicle on the 30 acre farm, which is something that the family has been doing for decades.

In the 80 plus years that the Carns family has owned the farm, they had never received one citation for their operations, that is until David Carns had a reporter reach out to Mayor Chuck Watson to ask him why he was stiffing David on the $450 bill for the firewood he delivered to the Mayor in January of this year. David dropped off wood to the Mayor on January 18th, with the Mayor promising several times to pay David, a promise that only came true after the call was made to the Mayor from the reporter.

Last year when the Mayor was up for re-election, he helped to change an ordinance to allow for properties that were properly zoned to set up roadside farm stands, which also included the Carns ability to sell firewood.

Two weeks prior to the Mayor taking delivery of the firewood in January of this year, the Mayor requested any complaints that had been made against the farm, a request that the Carns, and many others, found suspicious.

Since the March 22nd call was made by a reporter from the Pine Barrens Tribune, the family has received five citations and have been the victim of what can only be seen as retaliation by Township officials.

A couple hours after the phone call was made by the reporter to the Mayor, David Carns received call with a with a very disturbing message, saying only, "You're Fucked!".

Eleven days prior to the reporter calling the Mayor, a neighbor of the Carns, Sue McBride, lodged a complaint regarding a barn on the Carns property with Medford's zoning officer, Beth Portocalis, asking that the barn be demolished. Just a couple of days later a Zoning officer trespassed on the Carns property to take photos of the barn, which the Carns took offense to and let Portocalis know. The next day, two men showed up at the farm claiming to want to help the Carns remove the barn from the tax map, which is something that never happened, and the Carns believe, was just used as a chance to inspect their barn.

Just a couple of days later, on March 17th, the Carns received a demolition order from the Township for the historic barn. Then, on March 21st, while David was removing dead trees from a customers property, Portocalis illegally trespassed on David's customer's property and began screaming at David, alleging that he was cutting down trees in a wetland, while at the same time taking photos of David and his customer, who Portocalis also gave a citation to. David's customer testified that this is the first time in his more than 20 years as a Medford resident that he has ever been cited for anything, a move that has the resident extremely upset.

David Carns said that he and his family have been emotionally drained from the constant harassment, causing them to lose inches from their waists and hours of sleep every night. The Carns are no pushovers though, and they have been fighting back by showing up to Township Council meetings and telling their compelling, and frightening, story of retaliation by Township officials.

The citizens of Medford packed the house at the April 5th Township Council meeting, with several people chastising Town officials over their treatment of the Carns family. Brian and David Carns also showed up that night to tell their story and ask some questions, yet they left even more confused and frustrated by the refusal for officials to offer any guidance, as seen in the video below.

The Mayhem In Medford. Part Two: The Tyrant. 5-20-22

When a resident steps up to speak at city council meetings in NJ, they are asked to give their name and address for the record, something that seems so innocuous to most, so they just comply. They comply thinking that the personal information they supplied to the officials will only be used in good faith, for some type of record keeping or something, right? But what if they are wrong?

Rabble Rouser Media has acquired emails from Medford Township officials that show that the day after a US Marine, who is also a Medford resident, spoke out against the commercial truck ordinance, Kathy Burger, Medford's Clerk, sent an email to Mayor Chuck Watson as well as Councilperson Frank Czekay, letting them know of any complaints or possible violations on the two individuals properties.

In March of 2019, Kathy Burger wrote "The addresses for the residents who spoke on storing commercial vehicles are as follows: Mr. Buchler , 276 Tuckerton Road, commercial vehicle with crane on top. Sean Holmes, 244 Church Road, Tri-axle Dump Truck (Beth has received one complaint on this vehicle).".

Not to be outdone, Czekay writes back 40 minutes later, saying "Can you have Beth the 233 Church Road property to make sure the outbuilding in the backyard was built with all approvals and permits in place? It is a big building.". Burger wrote back, "233 or 244", to which Czekay responded "Sorry, 244.".

Both residents politely addressed the Council, sharing the concerns they had with the commercial truck ordinance. For that, they became the target of investigations by the town's Zoning Officer, Beth Portocalis, who herself resides in Pitman, N, nearly thirty miles from Medford. If these two were punished for being polite, I wonder how the Township officials would react if someone, let's say, stood up at a public meeting and called the Mayor a "Tyrant", as was done by Brian Carns on October 20th, 2020 when he and his brother, David, spoke out at a Council meeting regarding an ordinance that forced them to stop selling firewood.

The Carns family has been selling wood from their farm for several decades, wood that's gathered mostly from their tree service company, Cornerstone Tree Service, which was formed by their father with his partner under a different name in 1968. The ordinance they spoke out against in October of 2020, made it so they could not sell any firewood from their farm that wasn't cut from their farm, making those same trees that they have used for decades for firewood, useless.

As Brian Carns admitted at that same meeting, the Carns brothers are "a little rough around the edges", especially Brian. Brian and David are twin brothers who grew up in Medford their entire lives, helping their father and mother run their farm and tree service ever since they can first remember. The support they are receiving from the community is tremendous, with people cheering them on and chastising the Township officials, yet that hasn't stopped the harassment, and in fact, it has only gotten worse.

The Carns family has been dealing with issues with their neighbor, Susan McBride, since around 2016, when her and Portocalis began suspiciously texting back and forth regarding the commercial trucks on their property and other possible things they could be in violation of, which seems to have created NJ's own version of the Hatfields and the McCoys. McBride filed several complaints with the Township against the Carns, which in turn, the Carns chose to use their First Amendment rights by placing a sign by the road that read "Crazy Lady Ahead!", which didn't sit well with McBride.

On January 6th of this year, an email was sent out by Kathy Burger to Mayor Chuck Watson, with a picture attached showing an image that was captured from the Carns Private Facebook group showing the rear of the Carns family farm and their tree trucks. The email goes on to state that Beth "will be addressing the numerous commercial vehicles being parked on the farm.".

Section 501c of the Township's Code clearly states that "the provision shall not be deemed to limit the number of commercial cars or trucks used in conjunction with a permitted agricultural use", which is exactly what the Carns Farm is, so why is the Township taking enforcement action?

In the same January 6th email from Burger to Mayor Watson, Burger goes onto say that "the Carns sister, Heather Carns, is running a boarding and grooming business on the property.", and goes on to say "I want to make you aware that Beth will be sending a letter as they tend to reach out to you or post disparaging remarks about the township," referring to the Carns.

Two weeks later, on January 18th, the Mayor asked David Carns to drop off 2 cords of firewood, with the mayor letting him know that he'd catch up to pay him the $450 later. After a couple weeks, David texted to remind him about the outstanding balance, to which Watson apologized and promised payment, but the Mayor didn't follow through. David texted once more requesting payment, to which the Mayor again apologized and said he'd get the money right over to him, only that never happened.

On March 11th at 1:27 pm of this year, David received a message from Susan McBride, saying "Hi David. I'm going to be putting the house back up again in a month. Could you move that pile of wood for me please and we can work on whatever money you need. Please.".

Just three hours later, seemingly frustrated that David didn't respond within the three hour window she must have arbitrarily set in her mind, McBride sends an email to Porticalis, saying "Hi Beth, I am always the procrastinator so bare with me...I'm thinking I may have to file a small claims against Cornerstone to remove those large logs they left on my property. David doesn't respond to texts. Brian is being a very ripe Brian. I also, maybe would like to have you condemn their old barn which sits right on the road. The roof has been flying around for years, landing on the road and in my pastures. I know it's historic, but it's got to be replaced or torn down. What are your thoughts?".

The next day, on the 12th, David responded to McBride, saying "Ok, I'll let you know tomorrow".

One day later, on the 13th of March, David replied and let her know that it would be $1,000 to remove the pile, a price that McBride didn't agree with and fired back with a veiled threat, reminding Carns of her allowing them to park one of their trucks on her property to avoid any issues they might have with the township.

David let her know that normally a pile as large as the one in her yard would cost $2,000. And suggested that she just leave the pile for the next homeowner. Just three days later, on March 16th, McBride went to the Township building and made a request to have the barn on the Carns historic barn torn down. That same day, without the Carns knowledge, a zoning officer for the city illegally trespassed on the Carns property to take pictures of their barn, something they only learned of later through several OPRA requests made to the township.

Two days after the zoning officer trespassed, the Carns were approached by two men from the tax assessor's office who claimed that they were there to help the Carns remove the barn from the tax map, which in turn, would help them save some money on taxes. The claim of removing the barn from the tax map never happened, and the Carns believe it was only used to get close up photos of their barn, which were being used to try and condemn the barn.

On March 21st, while David was working in a customers backyard, Porticalis illegally trespassed on the rear of the property without the home owners permission, screaming at David that he is cutting down trees on wetlands, an allegation which was proven to be false. That same day, Porticalis sent out a letter condemning the barn, demanding that they either repair it or tear it down.

On March 23rd, feeling frustrated and confused, and not knowing where to turn, David decided to reach out to a local reporter from the Pine Barrens Tribune to share his story, a story that included the Mayor stiffing him for $450. Just a short while later, he gets a message from the Mayor, just saying "Call me right away", a call that David didn't make.

Three days later, on the 26th of March, David spoke at a budget hearing to let the committee know about how Portocalis trespassed on his customers property and maliciously cited him for violations that didn't exist.

On March 28th, David was working at a different customer's property, when he received a call from Portocalis, letting him know that she was coming over to inspect the trees that he was removing, and to let the property owner know that she was coming. David let the property owner know, but they still felt uncomfortable. When Portocalis arrived, she wised up this time and asked David's customer if she could enter the property rather than illegally trespass as she did two days prior, a request the customer granted.

Portocalis claimed she was there to ask questions about the trees that David was removing, which David said a 10 year old could see that they were dead, but she instead engaged David's customer, walking around the property asking if they had permits for work Portocalis, alluding to what might be possible violations.

Fed up, the Carns showed up on April 5th to let their voices be heard at the Township's Council meeting, where David would come face to face with their Mayor for the first time since the reporter's call. Interestingly, on the same day as the Carns spoke out at the April 5th meeting, Portocalis prepared a violation notice giving the Carns nine days to remove their trucks off the property.

The Carns went back to the next Council meeting, yet the Council still failed to answer, with the Carns promising to return every two weeks until they get some answers.

On May 1st, just two days before Council was set to meet, Medford's Solicitor, Timothy Prime, sent a letter threatening the matriarch of the family, 80 year old Carolyn Carns, with heavy fines and jail time if the tree trucks were not removed from their property.

When the Carns showed up at the meeting on May 3rd, they just wanted the Solicitor to answer the simple question of when they could have their trucks on the property, yet the Solicitor claimed they couldn't answer them due to an outstanding citation that was before the court. This shocked the Carns, especially considering they had never received a citation yet, and they were told to go to zoning to ask those questions, questions that the Zoning Board on May 18th said that they could not answer either, leaving the Carns even more frustrated and confused.

Since 2012, Susan McBride has called 911 at least 17 times, some being for requests for officers to help catch her lost ponies, others for neighbors who dare to try to use her driveway to turn around, and two very odd ones made that request police to be on alert about the Carns because her teenage children are home without her.

The Carns have also called 911 on McBride twice as well, once for her dog being loose, and another time for trespassing, with all four calls between the neighbors being made since the Mayhem in Medford began some two months ago when David didn't return McBride's text message fast enough.
With the Medford Council meeting looming next week on the 24th, the tension is building in the rural community, with many wanting answers. Many of the people on social media are wondering how a person who lives in Pitman, such as Portocalis does, can be harassing people who have lived and worked in

Medford their entire lives?

Our theory is that when you arm a BBQ Becky with a badge, especially one that finds that it is her good friend, Karen, that is the one seeking assistance, that Becky will use her power to cancel the Karen dissenter by any means necessary, even if those means are highly unethical, and most likely, illegal.

CHAPTER 13
"Karen By Design"

The majority of Medford residents were very supportive of my mission in the online FaceBook groups, and they were even more supportive of the Carns family. Dozens of residents were now demanding answers from the Council and Mayor on the local Medford FaceBook pages, which at the time, the main one had nearly 24,000 members. Joe Maggelet is the moderator of that group who at first was very supportive of me posting and commenting and posting articles, but after I began to question Mayor Chuck Watson's residency, because I got a tip he was spending more time at his Tuckerton home than he was in Medford, Maggelet banned me. This didn't have much of an effect on my reach though, due to the fact that there were other Medford groups that allowed me to post, so the pressure stayed on Mayor Watson even though I was banned from the most popular group.

A couple of months later Maggelet had another issue with Watson and the Council. So when they wouldn't listen to his now new issue regarding what Maggelet had regarding what he saw as overbuilding, he contacted me and said that I had free reign again to do what I wanted in his group of over 24,000 members. And that the Mayor was now open game! But just like with Mayor Catrambone in Delran, Mayor Chuck Watson had his own army of trolls who were ready to attack.

This time though, the trolls were more overtly aggressive, mentioning everything they could find to tarnish my character, as well as the character of Carns and any of our vocal supporters. They seemed proud to be ignorant, whereas the Delran trolls tried to play more coyly, with a couple in Medford that were just completely out of control. Little did I know at the time though, but several of the most vocal of Chuck's trolls, were actually just one person who has many screen names that fit her many personalities, Nicole Stouffer.

Stouffer was new to town in 2012 when she befriended Chuck Watson. Stouffer and other online trolls like Alberta Wolfe, began their plan to bring their Tea Party type of politics to Medford. Stouffer helped Watson and his crew of Tea Party Republicans get elected in 2012 by helping to oust the old guard with a similar campaign of online intimidation and harassment that they were now using against me. Only they didn't realize that their attacks are like porn to me.

I love to fight, it's in my blood, it's in my bones. A good shot to the face only invigorates me. It makes me know that I am alive and turns me into an even more persistent beast. If you ask my enemies what my best, or worst for them, quality in battle is? It would be that I can be as ferocious as a pitbull mixed with a piranha, or as subtle as a whisper, but either way the facts I present always cut like the edge of a razor.

So with the type of neighbor that the Carns were dealing with like Susan McBride, I knew I had to collect all of the evidence that I could so the facts would speak for themselves. This way Susan would only have herself to be mad at, and hopefully, she would just go away.

If I have learned one thing in doing this type of work, it is that a mirror is the best defense against the wicked. They cannot stand the ugly sight of themselves being dishonest or unethical. It's their own image of immorality that deflates the soul of the troll, or the dirty politician, and it's what I live for.

I really wanted to help the Carns family, but I knew that Watson had already circled his troops around their farm, so I had to act quickly. By this time in the story Stouffer had created a FaceBook group dedicated to shaming and intimidating the Carns. She was relentless, but only online, because quacks like her usually cannot explain themselves in a public setting like a council meeting.

Mayor Chuck Watson and the Council members were acting like they had no control over what the Township Manager Kathy Burger, and the Zoning officer, Beth Porticalis, were doing to the Carns. But I already knew from emails garnered from OPRA requests that their claims were not true. Frank Czekay literally weaponized the Zoning department against citizens for speaking at meetings, and other emails show Porticalis giving preferential treatment to a potential brewery , so everyone in town knew that their story was hogwash.

Another thing that Mayor Watson has in common with Delran Mayor Catrambone, was they both ran for office under the guise of being more transparent then the previous administrations, and they both had video systems installed to record the council meetings that are also live streamed. These videos would prove priceless for me, and very costly for the boobs who fought to have them installed, as you shall again see below.

The Mayhem In Medford. Part 2.6: Karen By Design Charged With A Crime. 5-24-22

It's not often somebody video tapes themselves in the commission of a crime to use it against themselves, but when they do, it is most likely a Ken or a Karen. The name Becky was somehow replaced by the name Karen about three years ago, which is the term used to describe a nosey ninny who will call 911 at the drop of a dime on almost anything.

"Hello, 911, What's Your Emergency".

"There are people using charcoal in the park to have a BBO!".

"Mam, I asked if there is an emergency".

"Didn't you hear me, they have bacon in the potato salad".

"Excuse me, but what is your emergency?".

"Ahhhhh, I am being attacked by black people with chicken seasoning, send the police, it burns!".

"Sending a unit.".

This is the slightly embellished scene that played out in Oakland, California four years ago when Jennifer Schulte, also known as BBQ Becky, decided to call the police on a black family who were just having a BBQ in the park. Schulte did such an amazing acting job, inclusive of tears, sobs, and false claims of being attacked, that the name Becky was retired to her prowess as if she was the Michael Jordan of frivolously calling 911.

While BBQ Becky was held for a 72 hour psychiatric hold, she was never arrested or charged with a crime, and never publicly interviewed or has been seen or heard from again.

The same though cannot be said for the neighbor of the Carns family farm in Medford, Susan McBride, who not only called 911 at least 17 times in the last 10 years, but she has also been arrested multiple times.

McBride has been arrested four times for shoplifting in Medford, all occurring after November of 2021, and multiple other traffic offenses, which include blocking traffic two separate times. McBride can now add one more arrest to her criminal resume, because just yesterday, she was charged with theft for stealing the Carns's no trespassing signs. The same signs that McBride ignored when she took a video of herself trespassing on the Carns property, even entering a building unannounced but the video oddly stops just after she enters the building.

Information gathered from an OPRA request shows that on April 1st at 5:11 pm, that same video was sent to the Township manager, Kathy Burger, in an email that just read "Feel free to edit. I don't video well, but my kids are good."

When a video is made and or a new version of it is created, a metadata tag is created that stamps the time it was created. If you go by the time the video was emailed from McBride to Burger, it should have been prior to 5:11 pm on April 1st, but it is not. The version sent to us from an OPRA request shows that the video was edited, just as McBride suggested for Burger to do, and it was done so almost four hours after Burger received the video at 9:09 pm on April 1st.

While the edited version was sent to us, an unedited version of the video of McBride obviously trespassing on the Carns property, was sent to the Mayor, as well as all Council members on April 4th. The very next day the Township's Zoning Officer, Beth Portocalis, sent several threatening violation notices to the Carns family, telling them to move the commercial vehicles parked on their property and giving them 60 days to comply.

The Township must not have read their own 60 day rule in their violation notices though, because suspiciously at the May 3rd Council hearing, Brian Carns was told by the Township Solicitor, Timothy Prime, that Portocalis nor he could answer his question due to the farm having outstanding citations. Both Carns were directed to bring their questions in front of the Zoning Board instead of Prime or Portocalis answering since the case was now in the court system. When the Carns went to the Zoning Board, they were told by the Board that they did not even have any mechanism to help them, so there was nothing the Board could do.

McBride can chalk up one more arrest on her record as well though very soon, because the Carns are headed downtown to have her charged with trespassing from the evidence that McBride recorded of herself that the entire Township's Governing body was aware of. When a governing body condones illegal activity, and knowingly uses it as a tool to harass a family by deputizing a person such as McBride, they are willingly giving McBride carte blanche to commit crimes while colluding with township officials to put the Carns family through a living hell.

Tonight at 7 pm the Medford Township Council will be meeting for the first time since we released part one of our series. Just 2 hours after releasing part 1, Stiffed Wood, the Council canceled the meeting that was set for that week, but that doesn't seem the case for tonight, where the entire government body will be on the hot seat.

Minutes from 5-24-22 Medford Council Meeting

Heather Carns Canavan stated she has a deep passion for their farm. Ms. Canavan stated she is here to talk about the invasion of privacy at their farm. Ms. Canavan stated there are disturbing videos going around about them doing every day normal business routines on their property. Ms. Canavan stated she feels she has to look over her back every day. Ms. Canavan stated she feels threatened by their neighbor taking videos of them but more disturbing is they are being sent over to the Township Manager and then to Council. Ms. Canavan stated on November 6th she had a church function at the farm and the neighbor was videoing that also. Ms. Canavan stated Mrs. Burger has the authority to squash these videos when they come in and instead sends them to Council.

Brendan Canavan stated he is equally dismayed by a neighbor who stood up a couple of weeks ago and suggested to Council that she was approached by someone in Council's Administration to collect information on their neighbor. Mr. Canavan stated it is disturbing a video of little girls riding in an all terrain vehicle and Bible school children on a hayride, these are the types of videos that should be shared with Council and maybe there is something not right. Mr. Canavan asked if maybe there is a vindictive administrator who is overstepping her authority and recruiting a nosey neighbors to video and try and get dirt on their neighbors then deliver it to her so she can deliver it to you. Mr. Canavan stated people are not allowed to video someone's private area, that is against the law. Mr. Canavan stated they are looking at the legal course to go after the neighbor and if the neighbor says they are doing what they are told by the Township, then that brings the Township in. Mr. Canavan stated they want to be treated fairly.

Brian Carns Mr. Carns gave Council a survey of their farm. Mr. Carns stated they were at a meeting and left when the Township Manager went on record, which he played the recording of, that it was the Construction Official who was on Township property and took the photos of the barn, the Zoning Officer had nothing to do with it. Mr. Carns showed the photo of the barn and asked how the Township Manager can claim that the Township land is next to their barn. Mr. Carns stated the Township Official trespassed on his property. Mr. Carns stated their tree service and farm are being targeted. Mr. Carns asked the Council to look into it.

Dave Carns Mr. Carns stated to the Mayor this is about firewood, it is about retaliation for him asking the Mayor for his money. Mr. Carns read letters he received from OPRA requests between Susan McBride and Beth Portocalis. Mr. Carns went over a timeline, March 16th the Construction Official trespasses on his property, two days later the Tax Assessor comes out and wants to inspect the barn to take it off the record and save them money, March 21st Beth trespasses on Mr. Lee's property. Mr. Carns asked if any of the Council looked into that. Mr. Carns stated March 26th he spoke at a Budget Meeting but there is no video of it, on March 28th Ms. Portocalis comes out to a property on Maine Trail and looks at dead trees, the next day she comes out and is in the neighbor's yard taking pictures of him.

Patrick Duff (Transcribed): Greetings, how are you? Thank you for being here, government officials, thankless job.

I'm Patrick Duff. I will not give my address, and I'm not going to ask you to give your addresses either. When I first enter the relationship with a town, as an investigative journalist, I make an offer. I emailed you the offer, Mayor, and you never emailed me back. I said let's just make this all go away. Let's make it easy, but that's not the decision that you made. Now you have had a bunch of OPRA requests coming in. I'm going to let you know that it was me doing the OPRA's for the last couple months, and I'm going to be doing them to a bunch of towns like you, and I'll tell you why.

Democrat or Republican, it doesn't matter, the machine is broken! Party politics, and partisan politics, is done. You get a council full of Republicans and it's corrupt. You get a council full of Democrats and it's corrupt. Nobody asks anybody else a question. If somebody from your own party smacks your face with a turd, you turn and look the other way, because your boss tells you to.

You had a psychotic person employed by your Township to go trespass on the Carns property. You actually all received that video. You received an illegally acquired video, and then you wrote citations based upon an illegally acquired video. And yet you did nothing about the illegal act the woman did? You are all guilty. You're all guilty of coercion, conspiracy, and if you ask me, this is a RICO charge. This is FBI material folks! Think about that you allowed a woman to trespass on a person's property, and you utilize that information to then harm them. You're like a mafia boss. (pointing at Mayor Watson) That's disgusting man. Yeah you know, you put up a deer fence, and I look back into this. Instead of taking down the deer fence when you're asked to. You set up a subcommittee to allow deer fences. Imagine that?

You had an email sent out from the crazy woman, that by the

way, let's be honest. She's been arrested numerous times in Medford. Four times for shoplifting, I believe at your Shop Right, and she was not charged? And that was recently. So I said to myself, well if she paid a fine the first time, yet the last three times it was dismissed. Maybe you employed her and said, "Hey how about we make this thing go away, just rough up the Carns for me" huh? Is that what she's gonna say? You better watch out. If she says that you are in some big trouble.

Trespassing on, uh, Mr Lee's property. Did you see Mr Lee up here? I guarantee you that Mr Lee has never had one negative information interaction with any government official until that woman walked on his property. Do you know what, I guarantee you he has PTSD from that situation. I'm gonna give you guys PTSD! You better resign. You should resign. You should all resign. You should resign, surely. (pointing at the entire Council and then the town manager) What happened in this township to these people...By the way I put the article up like four or five hours ago and it's got 2700 views. Your entire community has seen it. You are walking embarrassments to your community. You allowed a person to trespass, utilized that video to harm them, and did nothing. And actually, you did something. You went ahead and harmed them even further again each time they came and spoke.

In fact, let's put this on the record. Each time a person comes and speaks and gives their address, the Township manager sends it to the Council people. Who is, where is he? (looking for Frank Czekay) You had an email that came to you about 244 Church Road. A U.S Marine, that fought for this country to have the freedom of speech, and he utilizes his speech and you used it against him. You should be ashamed. You should be ashamed. OK, think about that, "he's got a real big garage in the back, go check it out"? You can't compel enforcement. You said yourself that you were not allowed to compel a zoning officer to not write a ticket. "That would be illegal" that's your words. (pointing to

Mayor Watson) So can you compel a zoning officer to write a ticket? No, you can't, that's also illegal.

What has happened in this town...Here's the deal I'll make. Leave them alone, drop the citations, leave them alone, and say sorry. Let's teach the kids, teach the children, that it's okay when you're wrong to say sorry. You know the worst thing you can do when you know you're wrong? It's to not apologize. You have the ability to apologize, you have the ability to drop the citations. You have the ability to stick by good honest people, not somebody who should be in a mental hospital that you employed to attack them. You deputized a Karen! By the way, I just have to state this for the record. That video file that she sent to you, somebody altered that video file so there's more to that video and we want you to send us a whole video so we can see her snooping around the rest of the property that you all saw! And since you saw it, you're all guilty of racketeering.

MEDFORD TOWNSHIP COUNCIL MEETING
June 8, 2022

Dave Carns Mr. Carns stated he is up here for a few reasons, one is it has come to his attention that there was work done at Hartford Crossing Park. Mr. Carns asked if it was done in-house or by a vendor. Mr. Carns asked who did it as he was going to donate his equipment and time for free and if this is going to be billed to the residents that's unfortunate. Mr. Carns stated the Zoning Officer is retaliating against him and his company because she is blocking him from doing the work there. Mr. Carns stated his company was brought up at the advisory board where Ms. Portocalis said to use Cornerstone and he went out there and spent a lot of time going out to look at stuff and for no reason at all he is not allowed to do it. Mr. Carns stated it is fine if the Public Works guys did it but if you are using taxpayer money that is going to be frustrating for residents. Mr. Carns stated the problem with Ms. Portocalis is she is texting his neighbor at 9:30 pm and that shows what length she will go to hurt him, his family and his business. Mr. Carns addressed Mr. Prime regarding a letter he received an hour before the last Council meeting, which talked about his company, removing a tree in Sherwood Forest where someone had made a complaint. Mr. Carns stated he did some OPRAs and found the person who made the complaint is fighting with the Township or Homeowner's Association over whose land this is. Mr. Carns stated the letter said he may have taken down a tree that is on Township property and you know it's not, as you have said the Township does not own any property there. Mr. Carns asked Mr. Prime to explain how they could take down a tree on Township property if the Township told this resident they do not own property there. Mr. Carns stated we cannot get answers, it is very frustrating and they will keep coming to meetings, there is plenty of evidence of retaliation against this administration. Mr. Carns stated Mr. Prime's bill was $145,000 to the Township and saw he made a maximum donation of $2,500.

Brian Carns Mr. Carns stated they are still looking at going to court with their mother. Mr. Carns stated he brought with him the 501C, this started in late 2016 and they have gone through the Council, Attorney, Ms. Portocalis, Mrs. Burger, Taylor Design and nobody has ever acknowledged once about the 501C, why the trucks are at the farm. Mr. Carns stated they have been keeping their mother out of this. Mr. Carns asked the Council to look at the 501C. Mr. Carns stated they could dismiss the tickets and write them to him and his brother as everybody knows that is who should have gotten the tickets. Mr. Carns asked for an example of who it would apply to if not them. Mr. Carns stated when his mother has to go to court that is going to cross the line. Mr. Carns stated it is going to be a mess, they are going to appeal they are not going into court and saying, hey we'll make an agreement to keep the trucks off the farm if you dismiss the tickets, there are no deals like that we are going to fight all the way through. Mr. Carns stated it is going to get worse for everybody if his mother goes into court. Mr. Carns stated if someone would want to reach out and talk to us so we can try and move forward, as he has not seen a relationship that can't be fixed.

Duff (Transcription): Good evening, how are you doing? My name is Patrick Duff. I'm not going to give my address for specific reasons in this meeting. But listen he's coming to you, you know trying to make amends here. I mean he filed a tort claim notice because you guys realize that there are three attorneys that are ready to sue the Township. They don't want to sue you. I've never seen it before. I really haven't. They have all the right to sue you for abuse of power, for trespassing on their property, for trespassing on their customers property. For literally a scheme to make these people's lives hell, and I can't believe they're not saying yes to an attorney wanting to sue you. They wanted to come one more time, that's what we're here tonight, to try to make this right. I mean what the hell is going on here? We were just at Braddock's. What a cool place. You have a great town. You should let cannabis in your town. Cannabis is not going to hurt your town, it's only going to help your town. I've opened seven dispensaries in California, and every single neighborhood I opened a Dispensary, made the neighborhood a better place. Every single one. So what's happening in your town, and what the next steps are, either you go to litigation which is going to cost you a fortune. Let's be honest your Zoning officer trespassed on a person's, Mr Lee's property, that's she has pictures of herself trespassing. Your Zoning officer and all of the Council received video of a person trespassing on the carn's property, and you did nothing with it, um, except for adding more violations on the Carn's property. So we're requesting a sit down. Listen, somebody at the bar just called you "Beer Drinking Chuck".

181

Mayor Watson: I'm sorry?

Duff: They called you "Beer Drinking Chuck". Is that "Beer Drinking Chuck" up there? Let's sit down and have a beer, man. You don't have to do this to these people, they're good people. I go around a lot to this town now, and I've spoken to a lot of people, and I can't find anybody to say bad words about them. So the request that I'm saying here is, Mr Prime, you're an attorney, you get paid for this crap. You don't need to pay him anymore. Let's sit down and figure this out and throw the violations out against the farm. There's no true violations against that farm. You know that.

I'm going to play a clip from a video from the neighbor, she's dealing with the police at this point. The police are coming out to her property at this point because she trespassed on their property cutting their lawn. Imagine that? If you're sitting there, and you're looking out your window, and your neighbor who you don't get along with is cutting your lawn! Would you be okay with that? Would you? Would you? Would you? Would you? (pointing to each Council member and the Mayor) You wouldn't.

So they called the police and the police came out (video playing) Let me tell you what she says, "he's having a temper tantrum because he's got to move his trucks because I'm making life difficult for him, because he wouldn't just move the wood." She told the cops that she's the one making his life difficult. You can't support that. You're supporting that.

Writing those violations and not not protecting your citizens from somebody that's trespassing on their property, Somebody who obviously has mental issues. I've decided not to say her name anymore, because I feel bad for her children. She has her children out videotaping these people and you're supporting that. Do you support that? Would you support it? (addressing Mayor Watson) Listen, Some people think you don't even live in Medford, and that you live in Tuckerton. Any truth to that? How long do you stay in Medford?

Mayor Watson: Excuse me?

Duff: How long do you stay in Medford?

Mayor Watson: I'll answer the questions at the end.

Duff: Yeah, I'm just saying people have questions, but the questions mainly right now are why are you bothering these people for absolutely no reason other than a crazy neighbor making complaints that you know has been arrested in this town for shoplifting numerous times? There's a video of her talking to a police officer for 17 minutes. The police officer said, "Listen, you called for a parking violation, we're trying to figure out what's going on". She then raises it to a up by saying her "children are in fear"! Please go check on my children they're scared of the dangerous Carns family. They go up to check on the kids, and you know what the kids say? "No we're fine we're just out here chilling". But your mom says you're supposed to be locked in the house. "No we're not scared". Chuck, let's get a beer, let's solve this man. You don't want it to go to litigation, and you surely don't want me to write another story.

CHAPTER 14

Beer Drinking Chuck

Nicknames can be a lot of fun, but they can also sting like a hornet when uttered to certain recipients. Growing up, kids would call me "Scruff" and for some reason I hated it. It had no real meaning, but when others realized what it did to me, they weaponized it. It wasn't until I was awarded the new nickname of "Pat Stuff", by one of the funniest humans ever to live, Geoff Krause, that the sting of "Scruff" began to wear off. Geoff would jokingly say that it was because I had all the right stuff, which felt much better than being a Scruff, so I rolled with it.

Memes are another way of assigning a nickname, or just digging under a person's skin a bit. Sometimes though, my sense of humor can be a little rough. Like when I put out a meme of Wendy Mitchell smiling, with the caption that read "Hi, I'm Wendy Mithchell. My horse teeth have venom". This one got some folks a little too roused up, and some of my usual supporters got mad at me. So I took it down to keep the public on my side.

Delran is not only known for politicians like Big Spender Burrell and Colin "The Kid" Rafferty, but it is also known as the home of the Underdog Lady, Suzanne Muldowney, who used to be featured on Howard Stern's show, and once stood atop the Burlington County Times building ready to take off in flight.

As a kid I had no idea that she was a secret superhero, to me, and all of the kids that hung around Hunter's Glen where she lived, we knew her as Mary Poppins. Now I don't know where the name came from, or who made it up, but we all knew that if you dared to say it anywhere close to her, your ass better get ready to run, and run fast. When you uttered it, it was like a bomb went off in her head, and all the kids scattered as she chased us through the streets of the apartment complex.

Some nicknames follow us from early on in life, others nicknames are earned later in life as an adult by how you are perceived. Which is why when I learned that Mayor Chuck Watson's nickname was "Beer Drinking Chuck" the big push to make Medford a brewery row now made sense to me.

It wasn't long after I began my investigations into Medford that I had a mole pop their head out of the municipal building to tell me about a new brewery set to open that was being given some preferential treatment, and possibly, some kickbacks. After looking through Medford's Council minutes regarding the new brewery, I realized that all of the minutes regarding the new brewery were all held in executive sessions, so they were completely redacted.

Medford's website had a major flaw though, because I quickly learned how to access all of the redacted closed session minutes to see them without the redactions, which allowed me to see everything they had done and were currently doing behind closed doors. I am sure that the administration thought that I bugged the Council room or something, because I just kept printing stories with information I gathered from those closed session minutes, crippling the administration. It wasn't until the beginning of 2023 that they'd realize their folly and have the flaw in their website repaired, but by that time it was already too late, as you'll see below.

The Mayhem In Medford. Part 3: The Medford Beer Summit. #BeerDrinkingChuck. 6-10-22

I have made it a little ritual that when I go to speak at council meetings, I find a nice spot to grab a bite to eat and try and get a sense of the local chatter, which many times, is about my stories. Two nights ago was no different when, just prior to the Medford Township Council Meeting, I sat down at Braddock's Tavern to eat some spicy Thai Shrimp and sip on a lovely craft beer.

When I asked the couple next to me if they heard about the issues between the Township and the Carns farm, the wife immediately knew what I was talking about, but the husband had no idea. When I told him the story about how the Mayor stiffed The Carns on some wood, he said "Who, Beer Drinking Chuck?" referring to Chuck Watson, the Mayor of Medford.

As a beer drinker myself, I saw common ground, and knowing that the Carns brothers also liked beer, the idea of the Medford Beer Summit was born.

I entered the meeting a little late, with public comments just getting underway, and a Medford resident was asking that the Council rethink their position on not allowing cannabis dispensaries, which is an idea that I wholeheartedly support . The speaker, who is a Medford resident seeking to open a dispensary in the Township, mentioned that Medford residents voted for the 2020 legalization bill at a whopping rate of 74%, yet the Mayor and Council said they still needed to wait to see how they do in other communities before opting in to allow them. (He has since opened in Mount Laurel)

Both David and Brian Carns spoke, and both were much calmer in how they approached the Council and Solicitor. Who at one point in the meeting, barked at David Carns "That's Mr. Prime", after David used just his last name in referring to him. David asked the Council who the town paid to clean up the trees and debris at the Hartford Crossing trails, which is a job that Carns had offered to do for free months ago.

Brain Carns asked to please either drop the citations against the farm, or to at least reissue the citations to the brothers so their 81 year old mother doesn't have to be needlessly summoned into court. When questioned, Watson and Prime said that they'd answer questions at the end of public comments, but never actually addressed any of the Carns' issues.

In doing this work I get little tips from everywhere, and one of those alleged that Mayor Watson, who owns homes in both Tuckerton and Medford, has been spending a lot more time in Tuckerton than he has in Medford, which caused this person to question Watson's residency in Medford.

When I had a chance to speak, I requested a sit down with the Mayor, and let him know that the guy at the bar called him "Beer Drinking Chuck"-- a name he didn't seem to deny when I said it three times. I asked that the Carns family be left alone, and let them know that the town is about to experience some extremely heavy costs due to litigation for their abuse of power, especially considering the Carns just filed a tort claim notice with the Township. I then let the Mayor know that a lot of people in town had questions, such as, is the Mayor really a resident of Tuckerton, a question that seemed to make the Mayor a bit uncomfortable.

Next to speak was Scott Duzcko, a friend of mine and fellow First Amendment activist, who pleaded with the Township's government body to explain just why they are harassing the Carns family. Duzcko spoke passionately, trying to appeal to the conscience of the members of the town government, but sadly, it seemed it just fell on deaf ears.

After the public spoke, the Mayor, and Council person, Frank Czekay, responded by only addressing the cannabis issue, as well as the issue of whether or not the Mayor lives in Medford, or Tuckerton, and again, for the 6th meeting in a row, refused to answer the questions posed by the Carns. Even though David Carns directly asked if the town paid a third party to clean what he had already offered to do for free, the Mayor claimed to not know the answer to David's question, and instead skirted the question.

Frustrated with their responses, and knowing that they wouldn't allow for anymore public comments just so Czekay and Watson could get the last word, I yelled from the back of the room, asking them how could they not address the issues raised by the Carns? Watson said public comments were over and tried to silence me, which in turn I told the group that they were "WEAK". Watson attempted to silence me once more, and at that point, I told them that they were like a bunch of bad comedians, and booed them accordingly as I walked out of the Council Chambers.

In Delran Township the Mayor and Solicitor decided they didn't want the insurer to investigate their unethical and illegal activities, so instead of contacting them on time, which would have triggered an investigation. They paid $300,000 from the taxpayers budget to Dunphy's Landscaping for very similar treatment that the Carns are experiencing.

Medford's insurer, who is also the same as Delran's insurer, can refuse and or deny a claim if it is learned that a government official abused their power and acted illegally, which we already know was done by Medford's Zoning Officer, Beth Portocalis, when she trespassed on both the Carns, and a customer of the Carns properties. So if in the course of their investigation it is found that one of the government actors operated outside of the color of law, and willfully abused their power, the claim can be denied.

The feud has been going on for several months now, with no sign of either side letting up, and each time the Carns speak out, more citations and violations are added to the growing pile. The offer has now been made to Mayor Chuck Watson to sit down and find a resolution to what has now been dubbed, The Mayhem in Medford, but for now, the ball is in the court of Beer Drinking Chuck.

The Mayhem In Medford. Part 4: Strange Brew. 6-13-22

The last time we left off in our saga now known as The Mayhem in Medford, we found out that Mayor Chuck Watson, also known as Beer Drinking Chuck, has a love for the stanky swill, a love that we also recently learned is extremely well documented.

As of today, the Mayor has 2,171 beer reviews on his profile on Untappd, which is a popular site where people review beers. Mayor Watson has two set locations where he enjoys most of his brewskis, The Mayor's watering hole in Medford, and a place called Compound East, which is the other property he owns on the water in Tuckerton. Of The Mayor's over 2,000 reviews, one of his favorites, who he has reviewed nearly 50 times on UNtappd, is Magnify Brewing, a small brewery who has been operating in Fairfield, NJ since 2014.

When the Township of Medford transferred their municipal offices at the end of 2020 to a new building on Union Street, the Council and Mayor immediately began discussing plans to redevelop the old offices and land, which are located at 17-19 North Main Street. Minutes from a December 15th, 2020 executive session meeting, that have since had the redactions removed, show that "Council discussed a brewery looking at the 17-19 North Main property. Discussion ensued regarding a redevelopment plan and meeting with the interested party.".

Just a month later, on January 21st, 2021, the Mayor posted his gratitude to the owner of Magnify Brewing by saying, "Delicious! Thank you Eric and my friends at Magnify" in his review of a Double IPA made by Magnify Brewing called, Sit Tight.

At the February meeting, just a month after the Mayor gave the owner of Magnify Brewing a shout out, Mayor Watson let the Council know during the executive session that "a brewery reached out to him to let him know about their interest in the 17 North Main Street property."

A month later in March, a resolution was passed to look into the "potential redevelopment of 17-19 North Main Street" but at the same meeting where they approved the resolution, the town's Solicitor, Tim Prime, mentioned that he was already working on the redevelopment plan for the property, making it seem like the investigation into the "potential" redevelopment, had already been decided.

At the April meeting, and over the next couple of meetings, the Township worked on creating a request for proposals for the redevelopment of the old Municipal Building. The Request For Proposals would finally be issued on July 25th, 2021, seeking a redeveloper for the Main Street property, a redeveloper that the Mayor, and the Solicitor, seemed to already have in mind.

Just nine days after the RFP was advertised, and in what appears to be a violation of NJ public contract law, Mayor Watson, and the township planner, Scott Taylor, admitted that they "met with an interested party for the 17-19 North Main Street Property Redevelopment Area." NJ Public Contract law states that at no time shall a government official disclose any information which could confer an unfair advantage to any potential vendor, and while we do not know what was conveyed to the "interested party" at the meeting with the Mayor and Planner, the very meeting itself, created the clear perception of impropriety in how the RFP process later played out.

The only bid submitted by the September 7th due date for submissions was the one from Magnify Brewing. And, without any hesitation or questions, a resolution was drafted to award the single bidder the rights to redevelop the property.

The resolution was approved at the very next Council meeting on September 21st, with Mayor Watson and Tim Prime, both praising the single bidder. Mayor Watson made a claim on the record that the RFP seeking proposals was first advertised over 90 days ago, which was completely untrue. The RFP was placed on July 25th, and by September 7th the resolution approving Magnify as the redeveloper was already being drafted, which is just 44 days after the RFP was placed in the Burlington County Times, not the 90 plus days that the Mayor claimed the town waited for bidders.

The redevelopment law that is being claimed to gain the massive federal and state tax breaks on this project, does not seem to fit the location of the old municipal building, as you can see below.

"Land that is owned by the municipality, the county, a local housing authority, redevelopment agency or redevelopment entity, or unimproved vacant land that has remained so for a period of ten years prior to adoption of the resolution, and that by reason of its location, remoteness, lack of means of access to developed sections or portions of the municipality, or topography, or nature of the soil, is not likely to be developed through the instrumentality of private capital.".

While the land is owned by the municipality, can they really claim that the former municipal building, which was located in the heart of downtown, has a lack of access, and or that private capital wouldn't want to invest in the property? It is prime real estate in a booming downtown with no real need to tap Uncle Sam for tax breaks by claiming that the place would not attract private investors, or is somehow in a desolate location not easily accessed, because both of those premises are completely false.

When the Mayhem in Medford first started with Part 1, Stiffed Wood, we thought it would only be a three part series. But with all that has been going down, we are considering a nice little spot in downtown Medford.

The Mayhem in Medford. Part 5: Trouble Brewing on Main Street. 6-24-22

Last year when the Medford Municipal Government prepared to move from the old municipal building to the newly constructed one, they began to plan what to do with the old property located at 17-19 North Main Street, a property that the Medford Municipal Government was still occupying until the end of 2021. The over 7,600 square foot building sits on a lot just slightly bigger than a half an acre, with 11 parking spots located at the back of the lot next to Charles Street. The assessment on the property as of last year was $890,420, yet the appraisals used to set the sale price are extremely far from the nearly one million dollar value placed on the prime piece of real estate.

At the July 6th closed session meeting, the previously redacted minutes now show that Medford's Solicitor, Tim Prime, let the Council know that they had received two appraisals for the property. He said "that the appraisals varied in value and the Township will take the difference in the two and ask for this amount for payment of the land." As soon as we saw that statement we did an OPRA request for the appraisals, and boy oh boy, did we hit pay dirt.

Just so you can get an idea of what the current market is like in Downtown Medford, a building located at 10-14 South Main Street, which has no parking, and is just under 7000 square feet, is currently listed for $750,000.

The first appraisal received was done by Martin Appraisal Associates out of Hamilton, NJ, which was completed on June 29th, 2021. The appraisal used several comparisons to appraise the property, some from as far back as 2017, with none being from the Township of Medford. The appraisal compared land sold in Cherry Hill, Mount Laurel, and Lumberton, with their certified opinion finding that the old municipal building was only worth $290,000.

The second appraisal was done by Sockler Realty Services Group out of Hightstown NJ, which was completed on July 1st, 2021. This appraisal also used several comparisons to assess the value to the old municipal building, with all properties in this appraisal being from Medford. One of the properties used in the comparison is located at 11 South Main Street, which is a 3,457 square foot mixed use building that sold for $360,000 back in August of 2020, yet somehow the appraisal for the old municipal building came in at $146,000, which is only 16% of the properties assessed value.

Since the Solicitor said that they would ask for the difference in the two appraisals, that means whoever is buying the old municipal property is only paying $218,000, which is a literal steal by any sense of the imagination, quite possibly, even a legal one.

CHAPTER 15
The $10,000 Fine

Municipal court is never really exciting. It's usually just one in, one out. Prep and process, prep and process, it's really quite boring. Trials rarely happen, and when they do, it's over something silly like the overnight parking ticket I was given in my town during my battles with Medford. While I love the town where I live, I hate the fact that they have a law that restricts people from parking on the street anywhere in town between the hours of 12 am and 5 am. Instead of just paying the measly $25 fine, I decided to fight what I see as a needless law and took it to trial in Audubon court.

While in court I watched the public defender tell a man who had more than a dozen citations for having trash in his yard, to just go clean it up to abate the issue and he'll have the tickets thrown out. The man was resistant, but ultimately the Public Defender appealed to him and the case was postponed so he could abate the issues, which is an offer that was never made to Carolyn Carns, who only had two tickets.

The Judge in Audubon is a man named Charles Shimberg, who is also the same judge in Pemberton Township where Carolyn Carns case was heard. In my opinion, and the opinion of many others, Shimberg is a major asshole and doesn't belong on the bench. He chastises people for things having their hand in their pocket while in front of him, or if he thinks you are not listening. He's rude, obnoxious, and should not be a judge.

I have seen my fair share of court rooms. It's fair to say much more than even some attorneys. I have represented myself at both criminal and civil cases, and I have never had an issue with poor attitude from the bench by any other judge like I did with Shimberg, as we'll get into later.

I knew Shimberg was an asshole, but as you will see below, I thought when Medford's prosecutor Christopher "Pig Vomit" Koustouris asked for $10,000 in fines for the first time offending octogenarian Carolyn Carns, there was no way that Shimberg would go for it. Or would he?

Medford Officials Seek $10,000 In Fines Against Carns Family. 9-15-22

Negotiations between the Carns Family and Medford Township officials broke down last month when the family refused to agree to two very strange conditions that the Township's team of attorneys, Tim Prime and Chris Koutsouris, wanted to include in an agreement that was set to be signed where the Carns were agreeing to not keep their commercial tree trucks overnight on their Medford property.

The first strange condition was that the Carns, who own a tree farm, a tree service, and sell firewood, could not split firewood on their own 30 acre tree farm that the family has owned for nearly a century. Second, the Township's dream team wanted the Carns to agree to inform the city of all of the locations where they were storing their trucks and equipment, which the Carns refused to sign.

The case is being held in Pemberton's Municipal Court due to a conflict of interest that the Carns have with Medford's Municipal Judge, Peter Lange. Yet Medford is still sending their Prosecutor to Pemberton instead of allowing for Pemberton's Prosecutor to handle it, as would normally be the case. If the Carns were to sign that agreement, they'd only have had to pay minimal fines and court costs, but since they refused to agree to what they felt to be unconstitutional and uncalled for conditions, the Dream Team of Tim Prime and Chris Koutsouris are now seeking $10,000 in fines from Pemberton's Municipal Court Judge, Charles Shimberg.

Information gathered from a recent OPRA request shows that for the last five years, the most any person who had been found guilty, or pleaded guilty, of any civil violation in Medford, has never paid more than $1,000 in fines. So why is it that Medford officials are asking for 10 times that amount for an alleged violation that was abated months ago? The commercial trucks have not been stored on the farm for months, yet they are still being vigorously prosecuted for alleged violations that no longer even exist. Why?

The point of civil penalties for local ordinances are meant to compel compliance in people who refuse to be compliant. But since the Carns have already abated the "issue" of storing the commercial trucks on the farm, what then is the purpose of the Township requesting massive fines? Is this about compelling good behavior, or compelling the Carns to accept some sort of guilt and avoid a malicious prosecution suit?

You see, if the violations against the Carns are thrown out by the Judge this Monday after he learns that the alleged violations have already been abated, the Township can be sued for malicious prosecution by the Carns, which is something the Medford dream team knows all too well. The fact that Medford officials are threatening the Carns with jail time and $10,000 fines, for what has never garnered more than a $1,000 fine, can only be seen as a type of extortion in order for the Carns to accept some guilt, which in turn, would make a malicious prosecution claim unattainable.

This Monday Medford's legal Dream Team claims that they will be stepping up and asking Judge Shimberg to fine Carolyn Carns $10,000 for issues that no longer even exist. But we are predicting that the bluff they played on the Carns never happens, and that if they do, we also predict the Judge will rip them a new one.

It is clear to anyone who knows the facts surrounding this situation that the prosecution of the Carns has nothing to do with commercial trucks being parked on the farm. The real retaliation only began after David Carns had a reporter call Mayor Chuck Watson to ask him why he stiffed David on $450 of firewood. This is not about compelling good behavior, this is about how an elected official and his associates can use their official powers to punish private citizens who they feel crossed them.

81 Year Old Carolyn Carns Truthfulness Mocked By Medford's Prosecutor For Going To Church. 10-18-22

Today was the big day in court for the commercial truck kingpin, 81 year old Carolyn Carns, who was in court facing two local ordinance violations for parking more than one commercial vehicle on her property. When I say that she is a commercial truck kingpin, I am being facetious, because anyone who knows about this story, knows that the 81 year old Matriarch of the Carns Family, has nothing to do with the commercial trucks that have been at the center of the Mayhem in Medford.

The trucks are owned and operated by her two twin sons, Brian and David, and the 81 year old, who is bound to a wheelchair and motorized scooters, has nothing to do with the vehicles that had been parked on the property for decades.

I could not believe my ears today when I heard Medford's

Prosecutor claim that the Township could fine Ms Carns upwards of $115,000 per each of the two violations, but instead he was giving her some sort of break by only seeking $5,000 per each violation, totaling $10,000 in fines. He claimed that Medford had proof that the trucks were parked there for 115 days, with his main witness being the Carns' old neighbor, Susan McBride.

In a true twist of irony, Susan McBride, who is the Medford Prosecutor's main witness to the trucks being parked on the farm, has a $1,000 warrant out for her arrest from Medford's Municipal Court for property theft from the Carns farm. There is no way that Medford's Prosecutor could not have known that McBride had the warrant out for her arrest. But he invited her to Municipal Court anyway to try and railroad an 81 year old woman who has never committed one crime in her life, while McBride has a rap sheet as long as her arm.

During the Carns attorney's opening statement, he let the judge know that Ms Carns has never been in any trouble with the law, and added that she attends church three times per week. When the prosecutor had a chance to respond, he mocked the 81 year old's faith by condescendingly saying "We have somebody telling the court they are in compliance and we are taking their word for it. I don't think Ms. Carns would appear before the court on the day of the plea, raise her right hand as a church-going woman, like Mr. Rosenberg said she is, and then lie to the court. So, if she is going to tell the judge that, 'We are in compliance now,' I am going to take her word for it.".

The Judge in the case said that he will rule on the sentencing in three weeks, which is when we will learn the ultimate punishment for Ms Carns, AKA The Commercial Truck Kingpin.

MEDFORD TOWNSHIP COUNCIL
MEETING December 6, 2022

David Carns – Mr. Carns stated he was here to talk about the fines that were recently imposed on his Mom.

Mr. Prime advised Council the Court notified them that the family has filed an appeal of the sentence imposed against them by the municipality in Civil Court as a result that appeal is still in effect and he has advised Council not to comment on the matter until the appeal is resolved.

Mr. Carns asked what they have to do with it except for having written the ordinance.

Mr. Prime stated he does not want any prejudice of any appeal for either his rights or the Township's rights.

Mr. Carns stated he is okay with Council not answering the questions, as he did not expect them to answer any. Mr. Carns stated this ten thousand dollar fine, he wants to make sure, as he has looked up a lot of records in Medford and the highest fine he can see for the first offense is three or four hundred dollars. Mr. Carns asked, isn't this a little odd. Mr. Carns stated someone who received a fine for a second offense received a fine of five hundred dollars. Mr. Carns stated this is his Mom's first offense and it is ten thousand dollars, something is not right here. Mr. Carns stated if anyone knew what happened between him and the Mayor regarding firewood, this reeks of revenge.

Mr. Prime stated he could not speak on it.

Mr. Carns stated the Township lawyer who asked for enhanced penalties against his Mom cannot speak now. Mr. Carns asked after the appeal will everyone answer his questions.

Mr. Prime stated they would have to see what they are.

Brian Carns- Mr. Carns stated he was here to speak about the farm and what has happened to his Mom this year. Mr. Carns stated the services have gone down and everyone has seen it. Mr. Carns stated this is the first meeting his Mom has come to and expected Council not to talk but the reason you are saying you can't comment is not true. Mr. Carns stated you can give your personal opinion of what's happened against our farm this year. Mr. Carns stated there is no judge that is going to decide differently with our appeal. Mr. Carns stated it would be great if his Mom could hear what happened. Mr. Carns stated she has nothing to do with the tree service, no idea about the trucks, she has never had a ticket in her life, she has never been fined and she has lived in Medford for a long time. Mr. Carns stated a ten thousand dollar fine is ridiculous. Mr. Carns stated Council could at least address his Mom out of some respect. Mr. Carns stated his fight has always been about the future of the farm. Mr. Carns stated it seems insane that Medford Township is putting this amount of pressure on a farm, we have asked nothing from you our whole lives we have been here, no preservation. Mr. Carns stated they try to run some small businesses over there and you have made it impossible. Mr. Carns stated there is nothing getting preserved in Medford, it has turned into a city and we want to protect and keep our farm. Mr. Carns asked why he has to turn into an activist to do that. Mr. Carns stated there is nothing like Carns vs Medford in the County or State going on. Mr. Carns stated there has never been any business fined in Medford Township for ten thousand dollars ever, small, big, corporations or little farms. Mr. Carns stated this stinks and does not make sense to us and the community has a lot of questions, everybody wants to know what is going on. Mr. Carns asked if anyone will go on record as they have told their side of the story, Council should comment or make a public statement. Mr. Carns stated they are not sweating it his Mom is on a fixed income so the most the Courts are going to get is twenty-five dollars a month, so it will be thirty years before the fine is paid off. Mr. Carns stated if his mother passes, the fine gets vacated so no one will get any money from us. Mr. Carns stated that's if our appeal over at the County is actually looked at from a serious matter with common sense. Mr. Carns stated no one has been fined in Medford like this before and he would like them to give him an example. Mr. Carns stated Mr. Prime asked for enhanced penalties and he is friends with the Mayor and this is what's going on, your mad at us and this is what you're doing, everyone knows it in Medford.

Jamie Wagner Ms. Wagner stated she was born and raised in Medford. Ms. Wagner stated she was here to support the Carns family. Ms. Wagner stated she thinks it is ridiculous what is happening and a waste of time and money. Ms. Wagner stated she does not understand and this is the first time she has spoken at a meeting. Ms. Wagner stated she sent the Mayor an email this morning. Ms. Wagner stated this Township is not what it used to be, the speeding, the trash pickup, leaves, trees being taken down with no notice and they are fined for taking down trees. Ms. Wagner stated she is here to support the Carns, as they are a good family. Ms. Wagner stated she can't wait to get out of town, this is political.

Tom Robbins Mr. Robbins stated he has lived in this town since he was a baby. Mr. Robbins stated the money that his family has paid in taxes seems to be going after the Carns family who he has known for a long time and are good people. Mr. Robbins stated it is awful, the Council really looks bad, and it looks very vindictive. Mr. Robbins just wanted to get his opinion across.

MEDFORD TOWNSHIP COUNCIL
MEETING December 20, 2022

Mayor Watson stated he has four statements he will read and after Council will have the opportunity to make any comments they would like.

Mayor Watson read the following Council statement concerning the Carns family. Like every municipality in New Jersey, Medford Township has zoning regulations, which were authorized by a 1927 Amendment to the New Jersey Constitution. The New Jersey Supreme Court has recognized that zoning is essential "to protect property values". The Carns family owns approximately

30 acres on Medford Mount Holly Road here in Medford. The property is farmland assessed which means that the property has a reduced tax assessment, and the property owner pays less taxes because a portion of the property derives income from agricultural uses on the property. In the 1948 Medford zoning ordinance the Carns' property was zoned A-Agriculture which permitted single-family dwellings, farming and roadside stands for the sale of farm products. The property is currently Agricultural Retention permitting housing at very low densities and agricultural and farming activities.

For over 75 years, the Carns' property has never been zoned to allow commercial or nonagricultural uses on the property. Yet for years, the Township has received complaints that the Carns have used, and continue to use, the property for its Cornerstone Tree Service business including storing and using commercial equipment and vehicles such as dump trucks and wood chippers on the property. The first violations occurred in 2016 and the Carns family applied for a use variance to allow the Cornerstone Tree Service to be operated at the property. The Carns family withdrew the application and agreed to only keep one commercial vehicle at the property and to not use the property for the Cornerstone Tree Service business. No fines or penalties were issued at that time.

Yet the Carns have continued to use the property for the tree service business and have kept commercial vehicles on the property. The Carns have advertised the property as the Cornerstone Tree Service business address. As the Township proved in court, the Carns have continually stated in public that they intend to operate the Cornerstone Tree Service business at the property. The Township provided the court with at least 8 instances that Carns stated in public that they were operating the business at the property. As recently as the last Medford Township Council meeting on December 6, Brian Carns stated in public that they want to operate their small business at the property.

The most recent complaint in April of this year resulted in the Carns being again charged with illegally operating the Cornerstone Tree Service business on the property and illegally storing and using more than one commercial vehicle at the property. On May 1, in response to a request from the Carns, the Township advised the Carns that the Ordinance penalties could be up to $1,000 per day and that each day of the violation constitutes a separate offense. The Township further advised the Carns that the Township would seek enhanced penalties because the violations represent a clear and unambiguous intent to continue to violate the law over an extended period of time and after the Carns had previously agreed to stop the illegal use of the property.

With full knowledge of the potential penalties, the Carns then plead guilty to both offenses and the court imposed a $5,000 fine for each offense, because the Carns were persistent and repetitive violators and could have been fined even more if the Township had requested it. Although they had full knowledge of the potential penalties before pleading guilty, the Carns have now appealed the sentence, which of course they have the right to do.

The Township Council is making this statement because its members are tired of being accused in public and on social media of being biased against the Carns and accused of seeking revenge against the Carns. The Township Council has remained silent while the matter has worked its way through the court process, but enough is enough. To make it crystal clear, the Medford Township Council has no bias toward the Carns family, none whatsoever. The Township Council is not seeking revenge against the Carns, in any way or in any manner. The Township has no desire to own the property or have it developed. When the Township receives a complaint, it is obligated to investigate it, for the protection of all of its residents.

The Township has occasionally had to inform other businesses that they were improperly operating in a residential zone. In every instance, except for the Carns, the business owner has ceased a violation. That is all that the Township wants the Carns to do: obey the law, like the rest of our residents do, to keep Medford Township as a wonderful place to live and raise a family.

Deputy Mayor Czekay stated he agreed with the comments Mayor Watson read and feels it is important to emphasize one of the last points regarding the Zoning Officer. Deputy Mayor Czekay stated the Zoning Officer is charged with the responsibility of enforcing the zoning laws, much like the Police Chief is charged with enforcing criminal law. Deputy Mayor Czekay stated we as a body don't have any authority over her ability to do that, we have delegated that authority to the Zoning Officer to enforce those laws. Deputy Mayor Czekay stated the Zoning Officer is the one responsible, we have to respond to complaints as they are received. Deputy Mayor Czekay stated we have said this a number of times that if we receive a complaint from a resident we have to investigate that complaint, we can't just ignore it based on anecdotal evidence as that person is crazy or that person doesn't know what they are talking about, we have to investigate it. Deputy Mayor Czekay stated if we don't investigate that situation and something happens the Township is potentially liable for what happens because we knew about the problem. Deputy Mayor Czekay stated the Zoning Officer had a duty to investigate those complaints, they were investigated and determined there were violations going on at that property and as a consequence of that the Carns were offered an opportunity to rectify that situation and they refused to do so and publicly refused to.

Deputy Czekay stated that is what resulted in them eventually being cited and fined by the Court. Deputy Mayor Czekay stated the Court is who levied the fine and could have said no fine even though they pleaded guilty, the Judge could have said I'm not going to fine you at all but the Judge fined them not the Council.

Deputy Mayor Czekay stated the statements made by the Carns that they could park at least one commercial truck there, he believes the ordinance says you can park a commercial truck on your property, the resident can park a commercial truck or the owner of the truck and his understanding is the trucks are not owned by the resident. Deputy Mayor Czekay stated that they may not be entitled to park even one truck on that property. Deputy Mayor Czekay stated they have made representations that they can park multiple trucks based on agricultural use but our ordinance says the trucks have to be either owned by the resident or used by the resident if not they can't be parked there. Deputy Mayor Czekay stated those trucks cannot be parked there because the owner of the property does not own or use the trucks, they are owned by a separate business that is run by individuals who don't own the property.

Mr. Rebstock stated he also agrees with the statement Mayor Watson read. Mr. Rebstock stated the challenge with public comment is challenging as it is comment not public debate and so they receive information and comments and choose not to speak back because of the situation. Mr. Rebstock stated we live here, we pay the same taxes, we share the same services and our ultimately neighbors. Mr. Rebstock stated there is no ax to grind, no vindication that they are seeking, they just want to live well with people. Mr. Rebstock stated in terms of the fine they were fined less than 5% of the total opportunity to be fined and believes that is more than fair and that was the choice of the courts.

Mrs. Kochan stated she also agrees with the sentiment of the statement and hopes that this statement provides some context and clarification to our residents. Mrs. Kochan stated we are all residents here and our goal is to live well with our neighbors.

Mrs. Symons stated she also agrees with the statement the Mayor has said and the other Council members. Mrs. Symons stated this has been a difficult situation. Mrs. Symons stated she was also on the Zoning Board for 9 years and many people wanted to do something similar and came in the proper way by applying for a variance. Mrs. Symons stated you need laws and rules for all residents in a community; it is not just for a select few or the few who wish to do it on their own.

Deputy Mayor Czekay stated there has been comments made that we are not business friendly, we are against businesses like their business but when he first took office in 2012 walking down Main Street it was a ghost town and today it is vibrant. Deputy Mayor Czekay stated our vacancy rate is probably less than 10% for downtown. Deputy Mayor Czekay stated we have looked at Taunton Forge, we have that in the process of being revitalized and we are looking at Ironstone. Deputy Mayor Czekay stated that all our commercial business areas have either been revitalized or they are going to be revitalized, so to say we are not business friendly he feels they bend over backwards as long as they comply with the law. Deputy Mayor Czekay stated they are ready, willing and able to help them any way they can to make sure their business succeeds.

Mayor Watson stated he would read his personal statement. I would like to once again address the firewood that I bought from Cornerstone Tree Service. I am tired of the lies about my intent of paying for firewood. I called David Carns and asked for a price on two cords of firewood. I never asked for it for free or expected any special treatment. Anyone that knows me or and even more so my wife, would know that we would never not pay a bill. She has planned to drive fifty miles to pay for a small plant that was missed at checking out at a garden center. That's who we are. He gave me a price that was agreeable and we set up delivery.

The first delivery was for the wrong wood, small chunks instead of logs. Days later the correct wood was delivered but came as I was walking out the door to a Planning Board Meeting. He said no problem, he would unload and we would catch up later. I was later asked to drop off cash, then a check to David Carns, then a check to Brian Carns all to be dropped off in the farm stand cash box. I wasn't comfortable paying a $450 bill in a cash box and I told David that. He said no problem, we would catch up. Several weeks later I was at a party that Brian Carns happened to attend as well. I mentioned to him then that I wish I knew he was there cause I would have brought him a check. We then discussed the wonderful photos he had purchased. I said I would love to see them and even offered to help pay for them if I could make some copies. We were supposed to set up a time for me to see them and I mentioned again that I would bring a check when we got together.

Then one day I get a message from Brian about an issue with the Zoning Officer coming to their job site. I responded: I quote "let's talk tomorrow, please send photos, I assume someone complained but I will look into it, she definitely shouldn't have done that in front of a customer in my opinion. I need to bring you a check to" end of the quote. Brian's response and I quote "hey thanks for the reply, honestly we realized the wood wasn't any good and would like to get you more this upcoming winter and go from there, hope all is well" end of quote. The conversation then turned to a violation they received on a barn on their property. I said I did not know anything about it and replied "can I stop by tomorrow?"

If that had happened I would have brought the check that we had just talked about the next day, that didn't happen. Hours later I receive a call from a reporter wanting to know why I didn't pay for the firewood. Apparently me being late paying them, which I have apologized for several times, would not have fit the narrative they wanted, so instead they went to the newspaper. We had just talked about me visiting the next day bringing a check and looking at the barn issue. Newspapers and social media have to fit their narrative better.

The next day I sent a check certified mail to Cornerstone Tree Service and we received notice that it was delivered. Before or since all this has happened I never asked the Zoning Official or any Township staff to go after the Carns in any way. I have quite frankly just tried to help them. I suggested the firewood being able to be sold and the Farm Stand Ordinance to Council that we all discussed and passed as a body and approved. Now they sell firewood and have a farm stand on their property, neither were permitted there before.

The accusations have been hurtful but I can sleep well knowing that my character and integrity are in tact with those who know me, maybe not to those who have believed the lies but I will work on changing that. Other than my mortgage I do not owe anyone in the world a penny, I pay my business and personal bills as they are received. By the way I never received a bill or receipt for that matter from the Carns or Cornerstone. If they had sent one I can assure you my wife would have paid it in return mail, she pays all the bills. Thank you.

Mr. Rebstock stated so publicly he has known the Mayor for 25 years and have had the privilege of working with his wife and son-in-law professionally. Mr. Rebstock stated he has known his daughter and son for that same amount of time. Mr. Rebstock stated he has also known young men the Mayor has mentored that have grown up to be fathers. Mr. Rebstock stated he can certainly speak and attest to his integrity, your concern for mankind, your honesty, just who you are as an individual. Mr. Rebstock stated he can vouch for all the things behind the scenes that happened with this that the Mayor spoke of. Mr. Rebstock stated he wants to point out one additional piece that he appreciated, that he was witnessed to as well as others, where the Mayor humbly stated an apology to the Carns family for firewood that was received humbly as well which was a wonderful moment for the Government.

Deputy Mayor Czekay stated he cannot do anything but echo the comments, he and the Mayor have known each other for 10 years and most of that time we sat on this Council and have always found him to be a man of integrity, honest to a fault. Deputy Mayor Czekay stated there is no question in his mind that the Mayor's intention was to pay them and was just a communication error going on that made it not happen right away.

CHAPTER 16
"That Kingdom Where No One Likes The King"

As a man who is on my second marriage I have learned that if I want to stay married, I can't say everything that I want to. I have a filter that halts me from saying things like "Why don't you do the fucking dishes", which if said, would cause World War III to break out in my house.

Not long after printing the Magnify Brewing story I headed over to my favorite local brewery called Tonewood to sip some of the best stanky swill one can find, only to see none other than Beer Drinking Chuck himself. I didn't notice that it was him when I walked by the front windows, but I did notice somebody's head turn violently as I walked by. When I realized it was Beer Drinking Chuck, I made sure to get a good seat so I could capture an image of Chuck sipping a cold one, and I got it!

I was being very critical in my online chatter of Judge Shimberg after he fined Carolyn Carns $10,000. I actually couldn't believe it, and luckily for me, I was set to go in front of him to have a trial regarding an overnight parking ticket just a couple of weeks later.

During the trial Shimberg wouldn't allow me to state my legal argument, and instead he interrogated me like I was a serious criminal. My argument was that the ordinance wasn't properly noticed with signs in town, yet Shimberg was grilling me and asking me if I was claiming that I did not know about the ordinance? Which was a ridiculous question considering this was now the third trial I had on these stupid overnight parking tickets in front of Shimberg. So he had to know it was a dumb question, but I know he just was trying to get me to lose my filter.

I was growing frustrated, and when Shimberg claimed I made a statement that I did not, I sought to correct the record. When I did so, Shimberg threatened me with contempt of court. I couldn't believe he did it, it made me furious, but I knew if I did what he wanted me to do, which was to tell him to go fuck himself, he'd of had the morbidly obese bailiff arrest me, so I didn't bite.

Chris Koustoris claimed to Shimberg that he was going lite on the 81 year old lifelong resident by only fining her $10,000, because if he wanted to he could have requested $330,000 in fines for two tickets for parking more than one commercial truck on the Carns family's 30 acre tree farm. He also rudely mocked Carolyn for going to church, yet Shimberg allowed it.

Just weeks prior to Carolyn Carns' hearing, a warrant was put out for the arrest of the Carns neighbor, Susan McBride, for missing her court date on theft charges she that got when she stole signs from the Carns property. The warrant was issued by Medford Municipal Court, where Koustouris is the Prosecutor, so he must have known about the warrant, yet McBride was present in court as Koustouris's witness against Carolyn Carns. That's right, McBride had a warrant out for her arrest in Medford, but the Medford Prosecutor was using her as a witness against the very family she stole from to get the warrant in the first place.

If you thought this shit couldn't get any deeper than this, put your waders on, cause we are about to go deep into some mucky waters.

Minutes/Transcript of MEDFORD

TOWNSHIP REORGANIZATION MEETING
& COUNCIL MEETING January 3, 2023

David Carns – Mr. Carns stated he was here to talk about the statements Mayor Watson made a couple of weeks ago. Mr. Carns stated there were some inaccuracies. Mr. Carns stated the first was the firewood and the Mayor said the reason he did not drop the money off was because he was not comfortable putting cash in the box. Mr. Carns stated there is a text message from him to the Mayor saying here is my address 265 Medford Mt. Holly Road you can mail a check out. Mr. Carns stated in another statement with our family farm and the commercial trucks you said in every other instance the other companies who were in violation came into compliance. Mr. Carns stated that is a lie. Mr. Carns stated there is another business who was fined $100 for the same thing and there was a second offense with this company for $200 and he was fined $10,000 as that was what Council asked for.

Mayor Watson stated you are here to address the Council.

Mr. Carns stated he will turn whatever way he wants; do you want to come down here? (Challenging Mayor Watson) Mr. Carns stated the third thing, there was a third ticket to this company, a tree service operating in Medford. Mr. Carns stated he wants to know why his mom was fined $10,000 and these other companies are getting fined $100, $200, $300 for second and third offenses. Mr. Carns stated the other businesses did not comply and that is the problem you treat them with a slap on the wrist.

Stephanie Moore Ms. Moore asked who runs the Medford Township page on Facebook. Ms. Moore wanted to know who wrote the post on December 21st on the Carns brothers. Ms. Moore wanted to know if they all agreed to put it on Facebook and saw it as a direct threat to the Carns family. Ms. Moore stated it was inappropriate and unprofessional. Ms. Moore stated enough is enough to what you are doing to the Carns family farm. Ms. Moore wanted to know why they restrict comments on the Facebook page. Ms. Moore stated maybe you should open public comments on your post so you can hear what people really think, nobody is pleased with you.

(Transcript) Duff: So at this point we're 11 months into this uh, you know back, and forth with the Carns family. At the December 6th meeting the Carns showed up here and tried to seek some answers, and Mr Prime you said that no comments were allowed to be made. You recommended the Council make no comments. Now at the very next meeting on December 20th, without noticing the agenda at all, four statements were going to be read in the record, one including the most controversial subject of all year, the Carns Farm controversy. And somehow the only people who showed up at that meeting, on December 20th, must have been told to be here, because they clapped at that statement very loudly.

It's probably the same trolls online who attack people viciously, at your behest, Mayor. The truth about the Carns Farm is, this is retaliation. It's a hundred percent retaliation. If it's not, then how is it the maximum fine that I could find for anybody else who got a commercial truck violation is $1,000? Yet you gave Mrs Carns, a first-time violator who has never been in trouble in her whole life, you recommended a $10,000 fine?

One of the people by the way, who got the $1,000 fine, I mean their record is weapons violations, violations of restraining orders, I mean, Jesus. I mean seriously, I don't even understand what is going on here at all? At the trial where Mrs Carns pled guilty you had Susan McBride, their neighbor, show up to testify. But she had a warrant out for her arrest that day from your Township for stealing from the Carns property. (Loud burst of clapping and cheering)

You hired, you encouraged a person who's obviously mentally unstable to trespass on their property. You accepted her video, and used it against this family. You not only should be ashamed of yourselves. That oath you just took, Mayor, that bible should have burst on fire when you touched it! (Loud burst of clapping and cheering)

You are not a good Mayor. You are a terrible Mayor, and you are terrible Council people for agreeing with this man.

The Magnify Brewing thing, come on buddy. You were in contact with them months prior to even vacating the building. You vacated the building and moved in on May 21st to the new building. But previous to that on December 20th you were talking to Magnify Brewing. Saying in closed session that you had "a brewery interested in the property" already.

Nine days after the RFP was put out, Mr Noel and you met with the representatives from Magnify Brewing. That's against public contract law. You cannot give them unfair advantage. You had the bid out for 44 days. You claimed, Mayor, that you didn't start the sales process for the building, in your statement, until after you moved into the building. That's a complete lie, Mayor. Why do you put statements out...but by the way. Why the hell would you make a statement after 11 months on the Carns farm, when Tim Prime told you not to make one? And then make it when the Carns aren't even here to respond. So obviously that's what is happening tonight, there's a rebuttal happening.

But here's what I think. I think that the fact that you Mr Prime that you Mr Rebstock, Mr Watson, you had mentioned that it was a judge that was the one that imposed that fine. Right? You blamed the judge. You said we could have asked for more, and you were nice to the 81 year old scofflaw, the commercial truck kingpin Carolyn Carnes. Right? You are criminals. If you ask me, you are breaking the Constitution. You just swore to be unbiased. You just swore on that Bible to be unbiased, and to treat your citizens with the same respect, each one of them. And look at the one you take advantage of. (Pointing to 81 year old Carolyn Carns in a wheelchair) Shame. Shame. (Loud burst of clapping)

Mayor Watson: Yes sir.

Brian Carns: All right, so like Pat was saying, we were here a couple weeks ago and everybody said you can't, well Tim Prime....Tim are you looking? Because you had a lot to say to my brother when we were here and you advised my brother and us, that you told the Council to not speak on the record, because this is under appeal.

Is there an answer we can get where that obviously had changed and you guys did go on public record with your statements without even putting it on the agenda for the night? You obviously invited your friends up. A lot of people knew you guys were doing it, because Alberta Wolfe is back there (Pointing at Alberta), I'm not sure who else was here. But there was some clapping over there. So you guys must go into executive session the night when my mom comes up here and we ask you to speak, and that's where you did your prepared statements. I don't know how else you would do it with Council uniting on this? So you tell us one thing there that night, and I guess then the following meeting you come out with prepared statements? Is that something like you guys could explain to me how that process actually worked, and why it wasn't on the agenda and it wasn't really explained to the community?

(Council and Mayor refusing to speak)

Okay. I figured that. Next thing would be, Frank, you go on the record and say that David and I don't even own the farm.

Frank Czekay: You don't.

Brian Carns: How do you figure?

Frank Czekay: 265 Mount Holly Road Road. You own that?

Brian Carns: I am on the deed.

Frank Czekay: You own 265 Mount Holly Road?

Brian Carns: Yes I do. I pay the bills there.

Frank Czekay: No you don't.

Brian Cran: How do you figure? I'm on the deed! I've been on that deed since 1983. My mom can't sell it.

(Mayor Watson tells Frank to be quiet)

Brian Carns: Oh Chuck, dude chill out man. Let him talk. At least somebody's up here talking.

Frank Czekay: I'm tired of this, I'm tired of this. He doesn't even know what property he owns.

Brian Carns: (gazing strangely at Frank) Are you wearing makeup?

Frank Czekay: No!

Brian Carns: First of all, there's something weird going on here. There really is. Something is weird going on here.

Frank Czekay: There's nothing going on here.

Brian Carns: I don't understand it. Okay? Are you saying that I don't own the farm?

Frank Czekay: You don't own 265 Mount Holly Road.

Brian Carns: How?

Frank Czekay: You're not on the deed.

(tensions rising)

Brian Carns: I am on a deed!

Solicitor Prime: There is a life estate. That his mom has, I believe but she does own, she has her ownership...

David Carns from the audience: You should apologize!

Brian Carns: You should recant your statement, because we do own it. My mom can't sell that farm without us signing off.

Frank Czekay: Okay? well then maybe we....

Brian Carns: Do you not know that? Do you guys not even do any research?

Frank Czekay: Maybe we should issue some more violations to these guys!

(entire audience goes wild)

Brian Carns: Bring em, bring em. Love it. Love it. (Audience still going wild and Mayor Watson is banging his gavel while Brian is raising his voice) This is what you guys are all about up here. Write those tickets, because you and Lauren, your seats are going to be empty. You guys are not coming back here this year. (audience loudly cheers) It's not gonna happen. Write those tickets, Dude.

Frank Czekay: That's OK, I'll have more free time.

Brian Carns: If you look into this, and it turns out I'm telling the truth. Where my name is on the deed. Will you go on to the public record and say you made a mistake and recant it?

Frank Czekay: You are on the deed? Do you have a current legal interest in that property?

Brian Carns: Dude, are you in a bubble? Seriously, you haven't looked up the deed at the farm?

Frank Czekay: No. I haven't.

Brian Carns: Did you know that our Grandfather wasn't even our mom's dad? It's our dad's father, he left it to all of us. The deed was left to everybody. We all own the farm.

Frank Czekay: At 263 Mount Holly Road you're listed...

Brian Carns: You guys, man, I can't get over this. My Grandfather left us this farm. and I got a member of Council going on the record, saying that I don't own it?

Solicitor Prime: What's it matter?

Brian Carns: It matters!!! Are you kidding me? I own that farm. I love it. And I have a public official up here saying I don't.

Solicitor Prime: It doesn't have anything to do with the violations.

(David Carns is yelling at Prime from the back about not being able to park the trucks on the farm)

Brian Carns: He also just said he's gonna write me more violations, right? I hope you're that dumb to write more tickets to us. I really, really do. Bury us, bury us with tickets, guys. That's how pathetic this whole group is. That's it. Happy New Year.

MEDFORD TOWNSHIP COUNCIL MEETING
January 17, 2023 (Transcribed & Minutes)

Frank Czekay (Transcribed) Before you begin the public comment, I'd like to make a comment about the January 3rd meeting. So if I can have the floor for a minute? I think we can all agree that with regard to the January 3rd meeting it was difficult for everyone, and certainly not a situation that should be repeated. I want to apologize for the comment I made that I made when I was interacting with Brian Carns, as well as to any member of the public that was present at the meeting or were viewing on the live stream. There is no reason why a meeting should ever deteriorate into the situation that occurred on January 3rd. We should all be able to have a rational calm discussion, and interactions that affect our residents, or the township. Even on those in which we disagree. So I yield the floor back to you Mr. Mayor for the public comment portion of the agenda.

Mayor Watson (Transcribed) OK, I think I pretty much think

I finished what the criterion would be. I'll echo Mr Czekay's comment about trying to keep decorum here. I don't want it to get into shouting matches like we had before at the last meeting, and we're not going to have it. If we have to take a break to get everyone under control again we will, but let's all just try to show respect for each other. Who's first? Yes sir.

David Carns (Transcribed) Good evening, my name is David Carns. I think you guys know that by now, I've been up here for ten months now.

You know Frank, you apologized but I got to tell you, I feel like it's because you said it on the record. I don't think you are sincere about that. If everybody looks out here (looking back at the audience) you are not going to see my mom here. Why is she going to come back here, she was threatened? She literally thinks that there is a letter or something coming in the mail, because that's what happened when we spoke at the other meeting. What was it, two days after the meeting, let's see, it was May 3rd or May 4th, two days later we were issued tickets, and honestly I'm not surprised you said it at all, because we've been saying all year that this is what's going on, retaliation.

If one of you guys got pulled over for speeding, right, and went in front of the judge and got a $10,000 fine when normally the speeding tickets are $100 to $150. Yeah, you might be scratching your head saying there is more to this, and there absolutely is.

By the way, does anyone know how much the Township has spent prosecuting the Carns family? Does anybody up here know? Because as of August, the Taylor Firm, the bill was over $6,000. That was up until August. So think about this, for the return, cause you're probably never going to get the $10,000, but for the return you probably already spent ten grand invested in prosecuting the family. So you are going to be at a loss, and now you have everybody, all the residents that think this is ridiculous. If they weren't sure, how we were being treated or why, after this $10,000 fine, nobody's ever heard of a $10,000 fine.

I'd love for you guys to tell me about another landscaping company or tree service that was fined ten grand, and I'll walk out the door right now! You won't see me again. I did OPRAs and everyone up here should. What you guys should do is look at the OPRAs and look at the other companies and say, huh? This company got 17 letters in a five year period. Right? Their first fine was $100, their second fine was $200, and their third fine was $1,000. Mayor, you sat up here four weeks ago and you said everybody went in compliance, and the paperwork that I have does not support that. I would like for everyone to look at this paperwork. Do the OPRA requests, send them to Kathy. She sees all the OPRAs we are pulling. Take a look at it and say, Hmm? Maybe we didn't know what these other fines were before we rolled out that speech and thought it was fair. Maybe everybody up here didn't have all the information at hand, and now looking at other businesses, maybe something can be done here. Because Mr. Prime, you can absolutely go to the Medford Prosecutor, who insisted, insisted, on being in this case in Pemberton.

You see Pemberton didn't have its own Prosecutor, most times when things are transferred they use their Prosecutor. But the Medford Prosecutor wanted to be a part of this, so he was part of this. It wasn't a Pemberton Prosecutor, like I've been hearing from a few people, this was a Medford Prosecutor. Tell me why you can't go to the prosecutor here and say, we don't agree with this fine anymore. Is there something we can do? Is it impossible to do?

Solicitor: Want me to answer?

David Carns Sure.

Solicitor As I understand it, your family, somebody entered a guilty plea, and you have filed an appeal to the fine.

David Carns Right.

Solicitor So the pending court case now, the Prosecutor is handling that on our half, and on yours I assume you are represented as well. We need to speak to the Prosecutor to see where this is. All I know..

David Carns Has anybody talked to the Prosecutor?

Solicitor I haven't. I don't know if the Council has?

David Carns (Transcribed) See this is how you guys get ahead of stuff, because we are pissed off right now about this fine, and if something can be done about it. That would be the right step in moving forward. Umm, yeah. I didn't want to spend a bunch of money appealing. We're not arguing up here saying according to Beth Porticalis, the trucks were in violation at the farm. Nobody is disputing that and we put the guilty plea in. What the problem is here is the $10,000 fine. I can tell you, nobody expected that. I talked to my attorney Friday and I talked to him Monday. Both days he said they can definitely vacate this fine. I don't even want the fine vacated. I want the fine to say what the other companies, if it was $100 or $200, then fine us that amount. Because just like you said Mayor in 2016 in an email, "everybody gets treated the same" and I don't see that here. Thank you.

Mayor Watson Who is next?

Terry Sheerin (Transcribed) My name is Terry Sheerin, I reside in Woodland Township. Kathy has been very kind to me about getting me some OPRA requests that I made, and I want to thank her for that. I worked all day today and I came here because it's important, because I don't believe any of you were raised to be bullies. Perception is everything, especially for politicians. Right now, you wouldn't want your children, your family, your spouse, none of them to be treated this way. We have a woman who is an octogenarian, she has been in this township for years, and she has done it unscathed. She's come through it and been a decent person. Regardless of what happened when they were kids, I don't care. Right now we are looking at a situation where that fine, to me, is excessive. I really believe you can go, you can instruct your solicitor to speak with the prosecutor and try to be reasonable about it. Come to the table with your solicitor, and with their attorney, and get it straightened out. I don't have a dog in this fight, but I see what it is and I used to live in a Township where people used to say, Medford, do you live in Medford? No, I live in Chatsworth, and people would say, oh OK. Medford was important, it's a little Hamlet that has so many things going for it. This is not one of those things. You are not bullies, and that's what your legacy is going to be with this. It's hard to say I have a transgression and I have to step back from it. But you know what, sometimes it's the way to solve things, and I appreciate you taking my comment, and (whispering looking at Frank Czekay) but it's a farm.

Mayor Watson Thank you. Who's next?

Brian Carns (Transcribed) Brian Carns, 265 Medford Mount Holly Road, that's my address, Frank! I heard your apology, but it doesn't completely make a lot of sense. I actually thought you were going to resign. I'm asking you to resign. You threatened my mom with more tickets. By the way, more tickets to us means, well if the first offense guys is $10,000, what's the judge going to say if we are back in front of him again?

Whether it's a joke or whatever reason you said it, umm, it's exactly what we've been saying you guys have been doing for the last 10-11 months. You could have called me any name, you could have said any kind of stuff, but what you say is "what if we issue you more tickets?". That's honestly one of the most truthful things I've heard from the Council in the last year.

So, you also talk about how the meeting was out of control, well I'm just a resident here. But you are part of the Council, you are leading the Township. I can come up here and act as crazy as can be, but you are supposed to stay professional. You are supposed to be looking, and that goes for all the Council. You are supposed to be looking after this town and what's best for everybody. There's nothing good about what's happened to our farm, our businesses, and our Mom! You guys have let this run. Whether you are part of it, or you are up here just letting it happen, we have been attacked from every direction.

The farm, Cornerstone Tree Service, I can't open Brianna's at four o'clock on a Friday afternoon because I get an email from Beth. It's crazy what went on last year. We were at a job and you guys are attacking the tree service and a customer. Let's just say, well a lot of residents would say "I'm not hiring Cornerstone. I don't want to have problems with the Township." But that's not what happened here in Medford.

The community understands that you guys are bullying us. You are harassing our companies, and last year was one of the best years Cornerstone has had in Medford in a long time. Thank God! Because this fight has cost us a lot of money. We've got to be, I don't even know, close to $20,000 by now with just fighting you guys. You guys are using our money too, and the residents to support your side of this fight when members of the community want nothing to do with this. They don't. I don't know how we have five people up here that agree that a $10,000 fine is OK for some trucks at a farm. When in the community, I haven't found one person that says, you guys asked for it, or this is what happens when you get fined.

So it's hard to believe, we do, we have five Council members for a reason, not just one, and you guys all share the same opinion when the rest of the community, as far as I know, doesn't? They just don't. They don't understand it and I think that you know, they maybe understand farms more than the Council members do up here, because if you guys did come out to the farm at some point, and actually looked at the operation there, and the idea of not having trucks there, it's impossible or very hard to run the firewood business. We have a tree farm there.

The state says we are recognized under farmland assessment,

which is only five or six hundred dollars, Mayor, on the record when you said we save money by being farmland assessed. There's been years we've been out. A lot of people opt out. They don't even want to be part of it. It's a lengthy application, and you have to come up with paperwork and everything else on your end to show that you are in compliance. So you are not saving thousands of dollars by being a part of the farmland assessment. I think at most it's been seven or eight hundred dollars.

But anyway, the state recognizes that, the Township should recognize that and say, OK. Well, what is it? If you have the firewood business there, and you have the tree farm there. I'm sure you guys don't recognize it as a big farm, and it's not a big one. But in a town like Medford our farm is a decent size. There's not a lot out there. So we do fit that mold. I imagine if we were out west or something, near farms that are 1500 acres, well it would look a little different. But in Medford, that is a farm, it is, and it's always been a farm. I actually think maybe a member or two of the Council should come out and take a look at what we are even talking about, because I do think that's what the community is so upset about. Some tree trucks at a tree farm, with a firewood business out back, OK, makes sense.

Last February this is where it started. The story should have been a crazy neighbor complaining, and Medford Township protects the farm. They don't go after the farm because of some...nutjob. That's it, guys. Reach out to my brother. We are not coming to any more meetings. We really want to chill. But let's keep the communication going and talk.

Frank Czekay (Transcribed) Mr. Carns, Can you stay up at the microphone for a second? I just want to say, and I want to say to you to, Mr. David Carns as well. My apology was sincere, OK. The words I stated were inappropriate, OK. They weren't meant to say that we were going to be issuing more, they were meant to say that if you were an owner the same violations would be issued to you as they were issued to your mother. It was not intended to mean that. I know how it came out. That's why I am apologizing for it, because it came out wrong.

Brian Carns (Transcribed) I am the owner and you should apologize for literally arguing with me for two minutes last meeting, suggesting I don't own the property. Why are you even bringing that up to begin with Frank?

Frank Czekay (Transcribed) I'm not going to debate that issue with you, we'll disagree on that. You are on the deed, there's no question about that. As to whether you are a current owner, or current legal owner, I'm not going to debate that.

Brian Carns (Transcribed) Dude. You should resign right now. Resign Frank.

Mayor Watson (Transcribed) Who's next?

Jatinder Singh (Transcribed) I moved to Medford about two and a half years ago. My name is Jatinder Singh, I am a CPA by profession. I moved here after my very young brother, a 23 year old, passed away. I bought a house on Mcanamon Road. It resembled a farm and my dad loved it, and I moved my parents with me.

I have heard a lot of things about the Council, about the Township, about it not being friendly. I came here to see today, this is my first meeting, and I am amazed to see. That's not what leadership should be. I saw the last meeting's recording, it was brought up, you know somebody talked about it. You know as a leader you are supposed to guide people. You are. We pay taxes. You know you all take that money and put it to good use for us. What I am looking at is that, residents here that are actually putting that money out for you to spend are being, you know, harassed, are being talked to..I know it Frank. You know you apologized, but some positions, you know an apology doesn't really do it, because you hold a position and then you have consequences for that. Now they are demanding you resign, you know, which it's up to you of course. Time will decide what you need to do, or you will decide what you need to do, but as a leader I feel like we should set an example for everybody.

We should make the best use of the funds that we've been given by the very residents sitting in this room here, and many out there. You can have differences with your leadership. You can agree to disagree. But you can't, people literally say, oh you're never, you can never get across to this council. That's not a good thing. I don't know any one of you personally. But to hear that, constantly out there, and then to hear what's going on in this room, it's really sad. It's sad.

I moved here, you know, I come from another country. I came here many years ago, but we came here for the American Dream. I'm looking at fairness, when there are issues, they are recognized. When issues are not recognized, and yes, you apologized a couple of times, I saw that sitting here. But the way initially that the apology started was not very well done. It started as if, you know, everyone had disagreements. Yes, we are going to have that, regardless, but it's how that disagreement was dealt with, that is the issue. So I think the entire Council, even for one person, needs to take responsibility for what happened last time. It's a joint effort. It's the leader.

Mayor Watson, if you allow it, that will happen. If you run your ship tight, and say this is unacceptable. I as a leader will take responsibility for that. That is your action to take, that's for you to decide, but I personally think that, if someone who is actually paying the bill, who is giving you the funds. One, this guy was told that, you know the gentlemen said that the state audits us. I couldn't find it, again, I'm a CPA and I've been practicing for a long time. I know when I look at audited financials. I had questions on that, but that is besides the point.

There are bigger issues here! I mean, your own residents don't even agree with you. How sad is that? How sad is that Kingdom where no one likes the King? I mean, how are you going to

continue living there? How are you going to gain that respect?
So I think here, the final blame, you have to take, Mayor Watson.
Whatever happened here, yes, Frank did something, but this is
your Council. You lead this.

What is your response? What do you think should happen so
you set an example so as to the next person will not be able to do
that? That's just my point of view. I come here, this is the first
time, and I hope this gets better. I hope we have a Council that
is for the people. Not a Council that is for itself, and is talking to
people as if they were their slaves, when they are not, and then
apologizing later? It doesn't cut it. Someone has to take the
responsibility and do what needs to be done to set an example
so it never happens again. Just my two cents. Thank You. (Loud
Applause)

February 7th Council Meeting

Alberta Wolf (Transcribed) My name is Alberta Wolf, as you all
know, I live in Medford. I'm addressing you tonight in order to
voice my objections over the one sided and unfavorable opinions
by what appears to be a small minority. During the past year
or so, I have heard repeated comments bashing this Township
and our Council. I don't expect to change any minds here, but
I've heard enough. I've heard enough of the negativity filled with
false and inaccurate information, and it prompted me to finally
speak out.

Ten years ago under the previous administration, Medford was
in dire straits. The town was run with impunity until we were
essentially on the verge of bankruptcy. Before moving here I
experienced close up, and first hand, what city and political
corruption was like, and I wasn't going to have that happen in
Medford. I began attending Council meetings, and as a new
group of people in town were seeking to oust the incumbents,
which is when I decided to get involved.

Two current Council members, Mayor Watson and Councilman Czeky, were both part of the transition to a more open and transparent local government. Initially due to our grave financial circumstances, they were forced to make very difficult and unpopular decisions. This included a reduction in labor forces in public works as well as our police department. This paid off over time resulting in an elevated bond rating, lowering our interest rates on borrowed funds. This all came with good financial responsibility and leadership. The budget was balanced, surpluses were created, and over the last several years road improvements were done, and the plans will continue.

We had purchased fire trucks, an ambulance, brush and brine trucks, just to name a few. All of this to better serve the residents of Medford. We were able to enjoy some of the best parks and recreation facilities in the county. We built a new library that was vigorously requested by the residents, and all this and more was accomplished without a need for an increase in our municipal taxes.

I used to hear that Medford wasn't business friendly, which was evident by all the empty shops and buildings along Main Street. A drive down Main Street today shows just how new businesses are coming to Medford because Medford is business friendly. Stores are occupied, space is in short supply. When weather permits, every Thursday is food truck night, and now the opening of Medford Mill has given us a big boost as well. New ordinances were enacted to open up the town to some previously disallowed businesses, and say what you will, but all of this has happened under this administration and their good leadership.

In regards to zoning, and the elephant in the room, large logos painted on the sides of buildings, or commercial businesses operating out of property zoned as farmland, are not permitted, and there are legitimate and rational reasons for this. Check the zoning ordinance in any township or municipality in Burlington

County, or for that matter the state of NJ and you will see that most have the same, or nearly identical standards. Those who chose to blame this Council for their non compliance are at best ill advised. Your time would have been better spent applying for a variance, and contrary to what some have insisted, an attorney is not necessary. So you can simply represent yourself. Much of the hullabaloo and legal action that has been in play for a little while might well have been avoided.

Regarding a well publicized zoning violation that ended in the courts. Most people are unaware of all of the facts of this case. The Plaintiffs have been fighting with the Township for years because they refuse to live by the rules. It finally reached a point where the Township was forced to do what it did because of repeated non-compliance and they handed it over to the courts.

The plaintiffs plead guilty, and the judge determined the fine would be $10,000. The fine amount is still under appeal but the plaintiffs want the local government to interfere with the judicial system to reduce it. Most people are weary about government involvement in law enforcement, but that is exactly what they are asking for. As with any violation, all they needed to do was comply with the law.

I find it puzzling at least, that two of the loudest voices who are constantly seeking to do harm to this community don't even live here. The administrator of a FaceBook page that seems to be sitting there at his computer with his devoted members bashing anything and everything Medford, twenty four seven, but he doesn't live here. Someone else who views themselves as a great defender of the truth, justice and the American way, who disgraces himself by attending our Council meetings for the sole purpose of insulting our town and our elected officials. This person not only doesn't live in Medford, he doesn't even live in Burlington County.

In conclusion it has become increasingly difficult to sort through all of the noise and confusion, to at least make an effort to learn the truth. Most people have only heard the constant drum beat of a small group of people who believe that if you tell the lie often enough it will become the truth. I respectfully submit that we are extremely fortunate to have such a focused, hard working, and honest group of fellow citizens running our town. My thanks to the Mayor and all the members of the Council for allowing me for this time to speak and thank you for your dedication to this township. To all of you listening, the truth is hard to swallow, so grab a glass of water and sit down.

MEDFORD COUNCIL MEETING

February 21, 2023 7:00 PM

Brian Carns (Minutes) – Mr. Carns stated nothing gets resolved when you do reach out and do have a problem. Mr. Carns asked Mr. Prime if he works for the Mayor or the public. Mr. Carns stated their problems started in 2016. Mr. Carns made accusations against the Manager and her not doing her job. Mr. Carns stated they had no idea their neighbor was spying on them until they did an OPRA and found there were videos. Mr. Carns stated the Manager should have called them when there were trucks on the farm and they could have worked it out. Mr. Carns stated the Manager is not doing her job and if Council wants to make some changes she needs to go. Mr. Carns stated someone did trespass on his farm and he told them about it and when he left the meeting Mrs. Burger stated that had not happened. Mr. Carns told Council to come out to the farm and he would show them where the pictures were taken. Mr. Carns stated he would like to see a job performance review on the Manager. Mr. Carns commented on the Manager having a new Tahoe and why she needed it. Mr. Carns commented on Alberta Wolf being allowed to come up and trash them and others at the last meeting.

Mr. Prime (Minutes) asked if anyone has harassed him or his family recently. Mr. Prime stated they were issued summonses, one for operating a business in a residential zone and having commercial vehicles there. Mr. Prime stated they pled guilty to both and Mr. Carns has asked for the fines to be reduced. Mr. Prime asked what does all that have to do with the Manager and being harassed? They have not issued any other violations. Mr. Prime asked what do you want them to do besides fire the Manager. Is there any other solution?

Mr. Carns (Both) Did you just hear me talk about recordings being made, secret videos by a neighbor with my nieces and nephews in the background? Mr. Carns asked the Council to not renew Tim Prime's contract.

Patrick Duff (Transcribed) – Good evening how you doing, Patrick Duff. Yeah, somebody came up here last week and spoke about me, Alberta Wolfe. She said I'm flying in here with a cape protecting truth and justice. If you look at the Philadelphia Inquirer today, the region page, I'm the front page of the region page. My research on Martin Luther King. A plaque being placed in Philadelphia, and tomorrow in Camden, so I actually do go from place to place, city to city and try to help people, and what is going on with the Carns family is absolutely ridiculous.

That's why I came here roughly a year ago now. To get into this, what do they want? They want the $10,000 fine reversed, they want to be able to park their trucks on their farm like they've done for years. The tree company started in the 60's, folks. These trucks have been parked for seventy plus years on the farm. You can't see them, right?

Now when the Mayor here, Mayor in 2007 you installed a deer fence on your property in violation of Medford's ordinance. Now you said that you got some sort of verbal commitment, but you never went out and got a variance to put the fence up, isn't that right, and the fence stayed up for seven years until somebody came out and told you to take your fence down. A Zoning officer, right, but you disagreed with the Zoning officer. Did you take

231

your fence down? NO! You stayed in continual violation. Seven years, by the way, at $365,000 a year, is basically how you fined them, $1,000 per violation, right?

So then you go and apply for a variance in 2014 so you can keep up your illegal deer fence. You say you don't do anything against the law? You kept the fence up for eight years in violation of Medford's law. Do you not agree? So, and then what you do is you lose the variance hearing. You actually lose the variance hearing, and then somehow after you lose the variance hearing, your neighbor across the street, who doesn't have a deer fence and still doesn't have one, came to the Council meeting and " wanted a clarification on what a deer fence actually meant, is a fence, is a net?" and you as a Council, you were one of the Council people (pointing at Mayor Watson), and Chris Buonii, the online troll that came and attacked me and everybody else on the 08055 page on behalf of you, stating that the Carns had no right to park their trucks on their property.

Well in 2014 he clearly stated that he was "All about private property, and what somebody does on their property is their business", and was very supportive of you and your illegal deer fences that stayed up for years. Then, not only did you lose the variance hearing, and have your neighbor come up and state some problems that you're having. But Frank Czekay actually voted against the ordinance, and you know why Frank voted against the ordinance for your deer fences? Because he said that it doesn't fix any of the problems that people purport to have. But you know who it did fix the problem for, (lookin at Mayor Watson) You, and only you. So you can keep your deer fence.

Now don't you think that is a bit hypocritical? You still have the deer fence, right, and you actually had the Township declare that deer fencing was not a fence, it was a net. When you purchase it, it says "deer fencing". The only spot in the country that considers deer fencing a net, is here in Medford to benefit one man. You should be ashamed of yourself, you really should.

You formed a subcommittee to create an ordinance to fix one man's problem. Your problem.

Now, as to Magnify Brewing. BTW what a great beer, I had my first one last night. Their beer called Monkey Business tastes just like Sunkist soda, it's delicious. But that being said, Mayor, you act like you can't do anything for people. You are walking into the auto shop and requesting that Magnify Brewing can have an agreement to use their easement. You are doing that on behalf of a business from Essex County.

Beth Porticalis sent them an email saying "Hey I got a great property for you, it's not zoned properly, you couldn't have a brewery there, but, the Mayor and you guys have been in communications for a while, and he also sits on the planning board." Mayor, you can do something about all of this. Listen, I have the inside track that some of you Council people met with the Carns and offered a variance for free to try and make it all go away, but that was in private.

You need to check your egos and publicly apologize to the Carns family. That's what they want, they want respect. Your deer fence stayed up, let's see, if we did the math like you did against the Carns family, what they said was they were in violation for 115 days. That means they could fine them $115,000 per violation, and there were two violations. He actually said that he could fine them up to $330,000. That's your prosecutor saying that, right? But he was going to be nice and only fine them $5,000 per violation. $10,000, the highest fine in Medford's civil violation history. Everybody up here made a statement and agreed with it.

Do you want to fix this? The way you fix it is to say "we're sorry, we messed up. You guys can park your trucks at the farm." They should be grandfathered anyway, 501c says that a farm can have commercial vehicles at the farm. But nobody wanted to answer the question 501c to the Carns, just like nobody wanted to answer this gentlemen's problem about $12 in taxes. Mayor, you are walking into private businesses and asking them to use their easement for a private business, and you are saying you can't help them?

These are your citizens. You're helping an Essex County business, and while they make a good beer, they don't live here. I don't live here. So I wouldn't expect you'd help me before you help them. But you are surely helping Magnify Brewing. You surely gave them a sweet deal. $218,000 for that property? I mean, come on. You're literally acting like a private realtor, showing people the meeting house, you are showing people the library, and none of these things are listed for sale, are they? That's not legal. This is not your town to pawn, this is not your town to piss on, with your deer fence and be an absolute hypocrite to people.

Medford is a town that most people want to move to, let's be honest, and this last year made it so a lot of people question that decision. I'm proud to be a part of helping people to question that decision. I actually made you a deal. You know, the guy down at Braddocks, he told me your nickname was Beer Drinking Chuck. BTW you struck that from the minutes. I said it three times, and you struck it from the minutes. You take yourself too seriously, Bud. Time to apologize to the Carns, ok? Have a private meeting with the guy. He tried to talk to you out there, you turned your back on him and walked away. Mr Rebstock came out and shook his hand and talked to him. You're the mayor. Be the mayor. Lose your ego.

CHAPTER 17
It's Good To Be The Mayor's Friend.

The saying "it's all in who you know" couldn't be any more accurate than when it comes to issues with the courts. It really is better to be rich and guilty, than poor and innocent in America, because the courts today are used more as a weapon to punish foes, than they are used as a tool to rehabilitate criminals. A law office in Cherry Hill has a sign out front that I love, which says "Just because you did it, doesn't mean you're guilty", which is a slogan Nicole Stouffer should get put on a t-shirt.

On October 27th The Pine Barrens Tribune printed an article regarding a recent Council meeting that mentioned comments made by Nicole Stouffer regarding the Medford Youth Athletic Association (MYAA) and her being issued summonses that caused her to have to get a lawyer.

As soon as I saw this I headed to the Medford Township website to find the video of the previous Council meeting so I could hear the whole story from the horse's mouth herself. Stouffer was there to berate the Township Police Department, claiming she was wrongly ticketed and screamed at "like a twelve year old boy with a beer" by a Medford police officer. Who then wrongly wrote her summons' for trash that the MYAA had left out. As soon as she started talking I could immediately tell that her tale was as tall as Jack's Beanstalk, so I gladly put on my Rabble Rouser cape and headed to the Opramachine.

The first thing I did was request the body cam footage from

Medford PD as well as any police reports. And just 10 days later my inbox chimed, and when I saw it was the body cam footage of Stouffer, I jumped into the air like I had just bought a new Toyota. I think I even did a little dance prior to hitting play, because I knew I was in for a show. Stouffer didn't disappoint either, hence why she is the final act in this real life soap opera.

I had a guy steal my car last year while I was showing it to him to sell it, needless to say, he picked the wrong guy to choose to steal from. I already had an image of him from the day prior when he first came to see the car, so I posted it along with other descriptions of him and what he was driving. The post was shared over 1,000 times in less then 12 hours in just my local area, and tips started to come in right away.

By 11 am the next day I had his name, and the name of his girlfriend, as well as a picture of the pair together, which I added to the massively shared post. Minutes later I got a text from the thief, saying if I take down the post, he'd give my car back. I said no to his request, and instead I called him by his name and let him know that I already knew exactly who he was, and I also had let the cops know as well.

He then told me that he was leaving it behind a McDonald's in Bensalem, and that he was hired to steal it by some guy who claimed I owed him a debt. I got my car back and he turned himself in, but shortly after he did I got a call from his girlfriend, who was livid that I put her picture up with his. She said her Daddy was the ex chief of a local police department, and that I would be in some type of trouble if I didn't remove it. I obliged but let the officer know about the call, which he acted like was no big deal, but I knew it was a form of witness intimidation.

He was charged with two class three felonies, yet he was released right away and never spent even a second in jail or was even cuffed. A couple months later, and without ever contacting me, the county downgraded his two felonies to one misdemeanor trespassing. Somehow the guy was not only marked as the victim on the paperwork, but he was also listed as a juvenile even though he was 31, so I knew some strings were being pulled.

A friend of mine and fellow activist, Jen Coombs, is a First Amendment auditor who takes video of public spaces, especially in publicly accessible areas of government buildings. During her audits she caught the ire of a police officer that just happened to also live close by to her who didn't like Jen filming. So much so that he sought a restraining order for her, which was then granted.

While Jen was filming at a public event that was being held outside, she came into contact with the officer who had the restraining order on her. Jen immediately left his presence. But unbeknownst to her, the officer went to the judge and sought to have Jen brought up on a violation of the stay away conditions, and a warrant was issued for her arrest.

Just days later she was performing her usual First Amendment audit by filming herself at the Lavallette Police station seeking to file an internal affairs complaint against an officer. When the clerk asked her for her name she at first declined to give it, but minutes later provided it when the clerk said she needed her name so she could get the forms that she was requesting. The clerk then gave her name to an officer on duty, who unlawfully accessed the criminal database system to check her record, which is where they found the days old warrant from Asbury Park.

The officers can be seen on body cam video accessing the records, and then walking into the lobby to arrest Coombs as she is trying to make the internal affairs complaint. Shocked, Coombs became extremely short of breath and needed to be taken to the hospital. From the hospital she was brought directly to jail where she spent nearly a year until her two separate trials, where she was found 100% not guilty of all of the charges by two sets of juries.

This system is broken. It has the same set of rules, but not the same applications of the consequences. It is completely corrupted, and the story below is clear proof that it really is good to be the Mayor's friend. Mayor's and councils hire the judges and the prosecutors that have the ability to take our freedoms away and fine us exorbitantly, or as in the case with Nicole Stouffer, just make it all go away.

Charges Dismissed Against Founder Of Far Right Wing Group Caught Red Handed Vandalizing Kids Sporting Complex On Film. 11-21-23

For the past three years Nicole Stouffer has been quite the busy little bee, fighting all types of causes. First it was the lockdowns and masks, then it was the LGBTQ movement, and lastly, and most close to home, her fight with the Medford Youth Athletic Association(MYAA), which has a baseball field that is right behind Stouffer's home that she feels wasn't being properly cared for.

I was first introduced to Stouffer when I came to Medford to help the Carns family, who in my eyes, and the eyes of many, were being intimidated and harassed by local government officials, mainly by Mayor Chuck Watson. Stouffer is a big supporter of Watson, who along with the Tea Party, helped him get elected more than a decade ago. And more importantly, Stouffer still helps him and his crew to quell any online dissent.

Stouffer's attacks on the Carns family were vicious, as well as her attacks on me, even going as far as labeling the lifelong residents, "The Carns Crime Family", and disseminating personal information she used to embarrass myself and the family. Stouffer even impersonated another Medford resident on the website www.opramachine.com, where she made requests for records for "The Carns Crime Family" which ultimately got her banned forever from the site.

Stouffer is the founder of The New Jersey Project, a far right wing group first dedicated to fighting COVID-19 restrictions, that has since morphed into an anti-LGBTQ/Trans group, focused on getting like minded people elected to school boards. Stouffer claimed that 68% of the candidates from 470 NJ districts that she endorsed, won seats in 2023.

Her online harassment of Montclair Mayor Sean Spiller even got her a visit from Homeland Security, where she admitted to using at least seven different screen names, something trolls like her do to build what looks like online consensus, when in fact it's just one narcissist shaping their own reality.

This brings us back to Stouffer's battle with the MYAA, and a post she made in May that showed a picture of a bunch of trash just lying on the ground next to a trash can. The post stated "There are parents here at the MYAA fields and let this happen. No one could walk over to the Lacrosse field and get an extra can? Does your yard look like this? Some of us take pride in our parks. Could you try to do so also?" But something was really off about the photo.

The photo looks like someone intentionally turned the trashcan over to dump the trash on the ground, and then turned the trashcan right side up again. The pattern of the trash on the ground matches the shape of where the lid of the can would have been if someone turned over the can. But who would do such a thing, and more importantly, why?

A couple of months later the Medford PD were asking themselves that same question when they found trash and other items strewn about in the street at the MYAA field directly behind Stouffer's home, so they began to investigate. They first went to Stouffer's home to see if she could help them access the video, but she refused, so the officers returned to the scene of the crime to interview some young men playing baseball nearby.

The witnesses identified a person fitting Stouffer's description as the culprit, so the two officers returned to speak with Stouffer, who for some odd or incriminating reason, had now turned her shirt, which read "Cocky" on the front, inside out and backwards. Police questioned Stouffer, who denied any involvement in the trashing, and instead attempted to deflect and ask the officers why the MYAA isn't cleaning their trash up.

Stouffer became indignant and told the officers they'd need to come back with a warrant, but the officers calmly gave her a chance to clean it up to avoid being ticketed, but she doubled down and refused. The officer then let Stouffer know that the MYAA has cameras recording the area, and if they showed her trashing the parking lot, he'd be back to ticket her.

Two days later the officer returned to give Stouffer four tickets, two for littering, one for disorderly persons, and one for leaving items in the roadway. Two months later the same prosecutor that vigorously prosecuted the 81 year old Carolyn Carns, Chris Koustouris, used his prosecutorial discretion to dismiss all four tickets against Stouffer even though he had her dead to rights on all four charges.

So the question must be asked. Why would Medford's Prosecutor so vigorously prosecute the 81 year old Carolyn Carns, insulting her in court, and imposing a $10,000 fine that was later overturned as being excessive, use his discretion to not prosecute Nicole Stouffer? Stouffer not only lied to the police, and can be seen on video committing the crimes, but she also went to a Council meeting and used the dismissal as her weapon to try and get the officer in trouble by falsely claiming he screamed in her face, when he was just doing his job.

With only three Council meetings left for Frank Czekay and Lauren Cochran, who both decided not to run for reelection, the

Council and Mayor are going to have some serious questions to answer at tonight's meeting, and the final two in December.

It was just last December when the entire Council and Mayor put out a lengthy statement supporting the vigorous prosecution of Carolyn Carns, claiming the $10,000 fine was necessary to keep order in the town. But now that they are faced with one of the Mayor's political pals who has not only broken the law, but did so on camera to try and incriminate the MYAA, will they have anything to say?

MEETING AGENDA

November 21, 2023 7:00 PM

Patrick Duff Hello my name is Patrick Duff. I am here to speak about the situation at the MYAA field, and also juxtapose that to the Carns situation here last year here on December 20th. This Council read a statement into the record. That you were all supportive of the $10,000 fine for an 81 year old on her first ever violation, that Mr, Prime, threatened her with jail time for. For parking commercial trucks that had been on the farm for decades, and juxtapose that to a person who intentionally goes to the MYAA field, trashes it, takes items out from the back of a shed and places them across the road. Takes a trash can and places it in the road, and kicks trash all over the place, and takes one of the wooden signs that has nails in it, rips it off and throws it in the middle of the road, and then takes a picture of it, and that picture she gave to you on October 3rd after her charges were dismissed by your Prosecutor who vigorously prosecuted Carolyn Carns, an 81 year old woman for commercial trucks on her own farm.

You have a video of Nicole Stouffer trashing your MYAA field. Your new Council person is a member of the MYAA coming on to this Council. You have created a monster. Imagine that, you have a person who commits a serious crime, lies to the police about it, comes up here and lies about the Police Officer. She said he screamed in her face, and you don't challenge her at all? You knew that video existed, and if you didn't, we need for you to make a statement.

You as a Council that made the statement last year on December 20th about the Carns. You said how you just have to be a good neighbor, right? Just follow the law Mr. Rebstock, you said "the Carns were only fined 5% of the opportunity that we had to fine them. But you know what happened is a judge overturned that fine, and you guys never made a statement past that. You just kept your mouths shut.

It is so sad that you have an 81 year old resident, that is a lifelong resident of Medford, right, that on her first violation you attack her viciously. The prosecutor during the court hearing, after her attorney mentioned that she goes to church everyday. He said, "well a nice little church going woman wouldn't lie now, would she?" Then the prosecutor requested a $10,000 fine that was later imposed. You Mr. Czekay said, "Well, it wasn't us that requested the fine", but actually it was. It was your prosecutor. The one you hire every year at your reorganization meetings in January, At your reorganization meeting, are you going to hire him again?

You need some changes here, you need some big changes. Listen, there needs to be something said by each of you who supported that statement last year. Who threatened people, Brian Carns while he made public comments here, with "coming out to the farm and giving you more tickets". This is heinous. Think about that, here's the question, what happens now? A video has been released showing Nicole Stouffer trashing the park that your prosecutor dismissed the charges of. It never went in front of a judge, they used prosecutorial discretion. He used his discretion. Did he have that video? He had to have the video.

Think about the difference in the two prosecutions? One woman walks into court and gets her charges dismissed without a problem. The other woman has him send her a letter threatening her several times. With jail time, massive fines, with all these other civil penalties. The craziest part is, that the same exact thing happened then. Their neighbor illegally trespassed on their property, took a video of it and gave it to you for the proof that you used to give them hell. So imagine that? You have accepted two different times now, illegally obtained material, of crimes being committed, and you accepted them to lambaste the MYAA, the Carns family, and the police. You should be ashamed of yourselves.

CHAPTER 18
What Happens Now?

Medford Mayor Chuck Watson and Delran Mayor Gary Catrambone have one more thing in common besides myself and that they are both up for reelection in 2024. Both ran on a platform of transparency. However, both are as transparent as a blindfold. What they used to call out from the sidelines as corruption, they now embrace as the corrupted, for power is the ultimate corrupter.

The $10,000 fine was the straw that broke the camel's back for the community of Medford though, because the pressure caused two of the Township's council people to request a private meeting with David Carns. David claimed that they offered to give his family a free variance so they can park their trucks on the farm without any issues just as long as we stopped publicly flogging them, which just shows that the Mayor and Council can pull some strings to get stuff done when they want to. Which is something that every one of them publicly said couldn't be done.

Even though Medford Councilwoman Lauren Cochran had just been named Deputy Mayor, she made the decision not to run for reelection in 2023. Frank Czekay also decided not to run for reelection, but that was most likely a party decision due the fact that Frank publicly threatened Brian Carns at a public meeting, but nonetheless, Czekay and Kochran are history. Brian Carns pulled his own version of my Swami of Salami, because he correctly predicted that Czekay and Kochran would "not be sitting there next year", and they won't be.

For the first time in many years a Democrat ran a very vocal campaign for one of the two town council seats up in Medford for 2023, Ray Coxe. Medford's voter base has roughly 1500 more registered Republicans as it does Democrats, which in 2021 was also how many votes the Republican candidates won by. But in 2023 Coxe lost by only just around 200 votes. Many staunch Many Republicans came out against the two new candidates, calling them puppets of Mayor Chuck Watson, and publicly stating that for the first time ever, they will be voting blue.

The Carns brothers are living testimony that all press is good press, because their tree service has never been busier, and on nearly every job the customers bring up the controversy. Many customers give cash tips to the twins just for them to give to their mother. Carolyn is still going to church and happily living on the farm. Brian and I have become good friends who have bonded through the battles we had at the council meetings and online with people like Nicole Stouffer.

After I released the body cam footage of Stouffer talking to the police officers, and turning her shirt inside out after the officers came back from questioning the witnesses. Stouffer released a long winded statement claiming she didn't trash the parking lot of the MYAA fields. The next morning an anonymous source sent me a copy of the MYAA surveillance video showing Stouffer committing the crimes, which I released as a fun little workout video, sending Stouffer back into the shadows.

Stouffer reached out to a person that we both know mutually, the bearded madman from the Atillis Gym controversy from the lockdowns, Ian Smith. Stouffer asked if he could step in to get me to back off, but Ian said that he told her that I am a warrior for anyone that I feel is a good person, and a menace to anyone I think is a crook and or doesn't like. He also told her that when he was being attacked by the media several times, that I was not swayed and remained a strong ally of his. Instead of Stouffer claiming to Ian that she didn't trash the MYAA field, she was more concerned with disproving that she was not the infamous Medford Pizza Pooper.

Ian said that Stouffer told him that I was lying about her being the one who allegedly dropped a turd in front of a local pizza shop that Stouffer and her crew had chased out of town a couple years ago. Claiming to Ian that it couldn't possibly be her, because she is such a shy shitter that can even take a good dump in a public restroom, let alone a sidewalk. Stouffer offered Ian even more proof by claiming that she still has Coleguard upstairs that has been waiting for some time now for her to drop a proper deuce on it. My guess is that even if we had a video that clearly showed Stouffer dropping trow and popping a squat to perfectly place the petulant poop on the pizza guy's pavement, she would still claim that the funky fecal facts do not matter. I can hear F. Lee Bailey right now at Stouffer's closing arguments as he says, "If the shit doesn't fit, then you must acquit".

Even though Stouffer had her charges dismissed, the public flogging I am giving her is worse of a punishment than if she were given $10,000 in fines, like Chris "Pig Vomit" Koustouris did to Carolyn Carns. Koustouris refuses to respond to any of my calls or emails, so I am considering going over to his office and pulling a Nicole Stouffer in his parking lot to get his attention like she did with the MYAA. I figure that even if he catches me on camera vandalizing his property, possibly even leaving a deuce at his doorstep to show my dismay, he will just dismiss the charges anyway because the state couldn't prove its burden, even if I was caught brown handed. That is unless of course I just happen to be a churchgoing octogenarian who has son's who have a beef with the Mayor, then it's my ass.

Stouffer's court hearing lasted all of 55 seconds, and Stouffer's attorney Michael DiCroce, who also just happens to be the Republican Mayor of the next town over, Shamong, lied to the judge. When Medford's Municipal Court Judge Peter Lange asked why all of the charges were being dismissed, Dicroce falsely responded "Because she's not guilty your honor, and once the state saw all of the evidence they realized they could not reach their burden of proof." And then POOF, just like magic, it all went away, or so they had hoped.

Because now it wasn't just me writing about the hypocrisy anymore, The Pine Barrens Tribune also picked up the story and titled it "Activist Takes Medford Officials To Task For Contrasting Treatment Given Carns Matriarch, Woman Accused Of Trashing MYAA Facility". And like myself, the reporter reached out to both DiCroce and Koustouris, but both again refused to comment, and something just doesn't smell right about that. Or is that someone's shoe?

The State had three witnesses to Stouffer trashing the parking lot, two videos clearly showing her doing it, along with police body cam video of Stouffer turning her shirt inside out to try and avoid detection after the officers spoke to the witnesses. Yet Prosecutor Koustouris couldn't reach his burden of proof?

Koustouris tied together a trail of lies to try and prove that the Carns were parking their tree trucks at the farm for 115 days after they were asked to remove them so he could impose as much punishment as he could against Carolyn Carns. But when Mayor Chuck Watson was asked to take down his deer fence, he not only refused, but instead of removing it, he had a subcommittee formed so he could keep it even after receiving numerous violations and losing a variance hearing.

Hey Medford residents. Show Chuck The Door In 2024!

My Rabble Rouser blog continues to put out interesting local stories that the news media are too lazy to investigate and write about. One such story is about a dog rescue called Lynn's Animal Rescue out of Evesham, where one hundred of the dogs that were supposed to be rescued, were instead allowed to starve to death in cages with a nine year old boy living amongst the squalor. I broke a story showing that just a year prior the little boy's sister walked into a 7-11 seeking help because she was living amongst dead animals, and while she was removed, somehow they let the boy remain.

In just 2022 alone I had over 100,000 views and 64,000 plus visitors on the site, which also goes by njrabblerouser.com. And while I might not have a cape and the ability to fly through the air, I have become somewhat of a political force through my blog and activism. A group of my friends have labeled me "The Mayor Slayer" for taking out Mayor Reid from Point Pleasant Beach. I am guessing that in 2024 I will be adding at least two more Mayor's names to my list, but that's not up to me, that will be left up to the voters of Delran and Medford.

I filed a lawsuit against the guy that stole my car after learning that he lived in a $375,000 crib not far away from where he stole my whip. The cop lied to me about where he lived, and the prosecutor told me a directive from Phil Murphy forced him to downgrade the felony charges. But just weeks later Governor Murphy signed two bills to enhance the penalties for car theft, which showed me that the County Prosecutor was not being honest with me either, so I named both the county and the township in a suit that I am waiting for them to respond to, which is why I am being slightly vague.

I am working with Seth Ferranti of Outlaw Films, who produced the movie "White Boy" that's currently on Netflix, and he directed Psychedelic Revolution, currently on Amazon. We are working on a documentary about my good friend who was murdered in California in 2005, Les Crane. Les was a pioneer in the legalization movement who I was introduced to by the Emperor of Hemp himself, Jack Herer. The movie follows the leads of the only remaining living witness all the way to the killers, but the cops are refusing to act, hence the need for the movie. The release date will be somewhere around 4-20-2024. www.whokilledlescrane.com.

I have learned that the pen truly is mightier than the sword, which for most of my life I thought was impossible for me due to what I thought were learning disabilities, only to learn on my own that the system was extremely wrong about me. I didn't read my first whole book until I was around 19. It was called A Journey To Ixtlan by Carlos Castenada. And even though it was kind of a silly fictional tale, I can remember it being life changing for me. Just as I hope this book is for you.

I am sure that my old teacher Ms. Schreiner, who made my life a complete hell in English class, will read this and think to herself "there is no way Duff did this by himself", as she does her snarky little lip curl and head bob. And guess what? She would be right. It was the teachers like her that gave me the inspiration to finally put the pen to the paper so I can show them that they were completely wrong about me. But even more so than that, so I could finally tell Ms. Schriener what I have waited to say for 30 years. Go fuck yourself, you Witch. Are you passing your old broom down to your buddy Wendy Mitchell? Because I saw you liking her posts about me, you old curmudgeon. (Extending both of my middle fingers to Ms. Schriener)

I dropped out of high school in 1994 with a GPA under 1.0, yet my testing scores on the state exams were all 90-95%. Luckily I did though, so I could go on tour with the Grateful Dead for a part of the Dead's last tour before Jerry Garcia died, which is yet another book in the making. I never attended any college, but I did go back to night school several years after I was supposed to graduate with my class so I could get my diploma to make my parents proud. Somehow I wound up giving the commencement speech for my graduating class, which while I do not remember it word for word, I do remember the gist of it. And it went a little something like this.

(A young extremely handsome me walks up to the podium)

"When I accepted the opportunity to speak here tonight I really didn't know what I'd say. But after sitting next to an 80 year old woman who is also graduating with me tonight, and hearing her story, I quickly realized what I wanted to say. We may not all take the same paths in life, nope, not at all, but sometimes we find ourselves at the same intersection, such as tonight. Some people didn't graduate so they could become young mothers. Some didn't graduate because they had family issues, and some were like me who just didn't try or who were failed by the system. But tonight, tonight we are all here together to celebrate this accomplishment. While our paths might not have been the normal path that most took as it pertains to education, that does not mean we didn't learn anything. Some of us were young mothers who learned how to love and raise a child, some of us were young people with family struggles who learned the value of hard work and perseverance, others had battles with addiction that they bravely overcame, but it made all of us who we are today. We learned about life, and then came back for the diploma. While most earn a diploma or a degree, and think that teaches them about life, but it doesn't. So I am proud to graduate with my class today, with the people who took a different path but met at this important intersection of life to celebrate our accomplishment together. Congratulations to my fellow classmates, and thank you all for your time. "

The crowd of all 40 or so people stood up and cheered as I walked back to my seat and sat down next to the old lady, who leaned over to me and whispered in my ear "Fuck Yeah, Dude", just kidding, but she did ask for my number.

Now please go leave me a good review on Amazon! Rabble Rouser, over and out.

Made in USA - North Chelmsford, MA
50054_9798871775172
12.26.2023 2151